One O'Clock from the House

A Comedy

Frank Vickery

Samuel French – London
New York – Sydney – Toronto – Hollywood

ONE O'CLOCK FROM THE HOUSE

First performed at the Berwyn Theatre, Bridgend, by the Parc and Dare Theatre Company on 3rd May, 1984, and subsequently at the Sherman Theatre, Cardiff, with the following cast of characters:

Miriam	Lynfa Williams
Josey	Helen Rees
Austin	Kelvin Lawrence-Jones
Tudor	Frank Vickery
Margaret	Iris Griffiths
Maureen	Elaine Andrews
Rupert	Damien Townsend
Mavis	Jackie Morgan
Avril	Pam Gould
Mansel	Dennis Stallard
Desmond	John Pritchard
Hugh	John Hingott
Warden	Irene Richards
Mavis 2	Carol Markham

Directed by Brian Meadows

It was subsequently performed at the Duke of York's Theatre, London, on 4th August, 1985, with the following cast of characters:

Miriam	Lynfa Williams
Josey	Pam Gould
Austin	Kelvin Lawrence-Jones
Tudor	Frank Vickery
Margaret	Iris Griffiths
Maureen	Elaine Andrews
Rupert	Damien Townsend
Mavis	Jackie Morgan
Avril	Deryn Grigg
Mansel	Dennis Stallard
Desmond	John Pritchard
Hugh	John Hingott
Warden	Irene Richards
Mavis 2	Carol Markham

Directed by Brian Meadows

CHARACTERS

Miriam
Josey
Austin
Tudor
Margaret
Maureen
Rupert
Mavis
Avril
Mansel
Desmond
Hugh
Warden
Mavis 2*

*It is advised when performing the play that **Mavis 2** should not appear in the list of characters

The action takes place in the living-room of Miriam's and Austin's house

ACT I   Scene 1 Saturday 5 p.m.
       Scene 2 Later that evening
ACT II Scene 1 Thursday morning
       Scene 2 1.30 p.m. the same day
       Scene 3 Later that afternoon

Time—the present

ACT I

SCENE 1

The living-room of Miriam's and Austin's house. Saturday 5 p.m.

There is a window UC *and a door* UR *which leads to the kitchen.* UL *is a door which leads to the rest of the house. The furniture consists of a stereo unit* R *and a large wall cabinet* L, *which has a door at the bottom, a pull-down flap and sliding glass doors to the display shelves. Downstage of this is a small table on which stands the telephone and a bowl of apples.* C *is a corner-unit settee, the type which has two seats, a display corner and a single seat. A small table is set beside the single seat and* R *of this is a matching armchair. There is a coffee-table in front of the settee*

When the CURTAIN *rises there is no-one on stage. Miriam enters from upstairs. She appears to be upset, crying into her hanky. She expects her husband, Austin, to be in the room*

Miriam (*breaking her heart*) Austin. (*She moves to the settee and puts her hand on the back of it for support. Calling*) Austin. (*She expects him to be sitting to her extreme left. When she gets no reply she looks in that direction. Seeing he is not there she looks immediately towards the armchair. Not there either. She drops her upset façade. Calling, with a touch of anger*) Austin! (*She marches towards the kitchen and peers off*) He's never left me on my own. (*Coming back into the room, realizing that he has*) I'll kill him.

Suddenly, the front door slams and Miriam dives for the settee and resumes her crying

Josey, her daughter enters. She is about sixteen, not quite punk but almost. She crosses to the kitchen almost immediately, catching sight of her mother as she goes. She screams the following line on her way into the room but is in the kitchen by the time she finishes it

Josey Oh, you're up then. Good. Feeling better?
Miriam No, not really. I've only got up now because——
Josey (*off*) Any hot water here, Mam, 'cos I want to have a bath?
Miriam Callous little cow. (*She spots a piece of fluff on her dress and brushes it away*)

*Josey enters from the kitchen carrying a hair-dryer, shampoo, towel, etc.
She moves towards the armchair*

*Miriam is not aware that Josey is in the room. When she looks up and sees her
she immediately starts crying again*

Josey Come on, Mam. (*She puts her things down on the chair and sits on the
arm*) It'll be all right.
Miriam I was his favourite daughter. And I wasn't even there when he went.
Josey It was you who insisted on going to the Bring and Buy.
Miriam I'd worked so hard for it. Audrey Cocklesworth was just dying to
replace me. Your grandfather's been on his death-bed for weeks. The least
he could have done was to have hung on.
Josey Oh the least. *And* seeing as you were his favourite.
Miriam Trust Margaret to be there. She's not even close to him.
Josey She *is* his daughter.
Miriam I was with him all the night before. Why couldn't he have gone
then?
Josey Grandad always had the inconsiderate streak.
Miriam And I don't know where your father is. The doctor said I shouldn't
be left.
Josey Doctor?
Miriam I had to call him out. To give me something to calm me down.
Josey They don't seem to be working.
Miriam Well I haven't taken them, you know me I won't take tablets.
Josey I must admit, you're taking it far worse than I'd thought.
Miriam It's a wrench, Josey. You'll never know. Your grandfather did very
well to manage that house on his own. Maureen helped of course.
Margaret could have done a lot more but wouldn't, and Mavis, (*rising
and moving downstage*) well, Mavis was a little bit crazy even then. No,
not crazy. Perhaps that's the wrong word. She's not crazy. She's cuckoo.
Josey You mean mentally sub-normal.
Miriam Yes that's right. (*Blowing her nose*) Cuckoo.
Josey What does she look like, Mam. I'd love to see her.
Miriam I don't suppose *I'd* recognize her now. She's been in that place for
years.
Josey Will you be having her out for the funeral?
Miriam For the whole weekend probably.
Josey Shall I make arrangements to stay with a friend then?
Miriam (*firmly; moving towards Josey*) Mavis isn't coming here.
Josey I thought you said she did the last time.
Miriam Yes. And I almost ended up back in that hospital with her. No.
Margaret can have her.
Josey I thought Margaret was having Grandad.
Miriam (*moving away*) She is. (*There is a slight pause in which she turns to
look at Josey*) Well he can hardly come here.
Josey What about the chapel of rest?
Miriam He always said to me, "Miriam, if anything ever happens to me,

don't you put me in the chapel of rest. I want to go from the house." And I'm going to see that he has his wish.

Josey Margaret's the nervous type. I never thought she'd agree to have Grandad there.

Miriam She's the only one who's got a front room.

Josey What about us?

Miriam It hasn't been papered. And I'm not moving that walnut cabinet for anyone. (*She moves away towards the cabinet*)

Josey What did she say?

Miriam Who?

Josey Margaret. About having Grandad.

Miriam We're having a meeting about it, here, tonight.

Josey You mean she doesn't know yet? (*She laughs*) I think I'll stay in, it'll be more fun than the disco.

Miriam She'll have to have him. I can't see any other alternative. This is no time for us girls to quarrel. We've all got to stick together.

Josey I think it's a bit unfair to expect Margaret to have Grandad *and* Mavis.

Miriam (*firmly*) Go and run your water.

Josey What about Maureen?

Miriam Her and Desmond are going through a sticky patch. I reckon your grandfather will just about finish them off. And Mavis certainly will. (*Moving towards Josey*) Besides, they've got the builders in. They're having a repair grant. (*Sitting*) And Maureen has done enough for this family over the years. It's about time Margaret did her bit.

There is a pause

Josey (*tentatively*) Did Grandad leave a will?

Miriam He left a letter.

Josey To who?

Miriam Me. To be opened in the presence of the other girls.

Josey What does it say?

Miriam That I'm to handle it ... well we don't know yet. It has to be opened when we're all together.

Josey Do you think he's left me anything?

Miriam You'll just have to wait and see.

Josey Shouldn't I be here tonight? I mean I am a grandchild.

Miriam The letter is addressed to me. But don't worry, if there is anything coming to you——

Josey tries to interrupt

—which I doubt—it will be kept safe for you until you're twenty-one.

Josey (*shouting*) Eighteen.

Miriam (*shouting back*) That bath will be flooded.

Josey (*shouting even louder*) I haven't run it yet. (*After a slight pause*) I wonder who'll have the house. I suppose it'll be split four ways. A wall each. Heaven help us when you get to the roof.

Miriam (*after a slight pause*) It might all come to me. Apart from Mavis, I am the youngest. And he always said the house would be mine.

Josey I never knew that.

Miriam Oh yes. That's why he gave the letter to *me*. It's all written down in black and white.

Josey So you get the lot?

Miriam Well we don't know for definite. Not until the letter is read. I'm only going by what your grandfather told me.

Josey (*rising*) I'm sure Margaret isn't going to like it.

Miriam Then Margaret is just going to have to lump it.

Josey (*leaning on the back of the settee*) When did Grandad tell you that you are to have it all?

Miriam A couple of weeks ago.

Josey Well that doesn't mean anything. He's been gaga for months.

Miriam Don't speak like that about your grandfather. He was only incontinent.

Josey His brain was incontinent.

Miriam He knew who I was right up to the end.

Josey Only because you'd never let him forget you. You kept feeding him your name every two minutes. (*Leaning towards Miriam*) Hello Father, this is Miriam here. Miriam. The youngest. The baby. Shall Miriam get you something to drink? Fetch the nurse? Change the flowers? Shall Miriam peel you a grape? (*She collapses with laughter on Miriam*)

Miriam (*pushing her off*) Stop it.

Josey (*still laughing*) And it all proved to be a complete and utter waste of time, because with his dying breath he whispered—"Maureen".

The telephone rings

Miriam (*getting up to answer the telephone*) I didn't mind that. I didn't mind that at all. He could have whispered any name he wanted—except Margaret's. (*Answering the telephone*) Hello? . . . Speaking. . . . From where? . . . (*She puts her hand over the receiver; to Josey*) It's Margaret. (*Into the telephone*) Yes, Operator, I'll accept the charge. (*To Josey*) She'd skin a flea for a halfpenny. (*Into the telephone*) Hello? . . . Yes I thought it was you. What's the matter with your own phone? . . . Well would you like me to report it for you? (*She winks at Josey*) Are you sure? . . . I don't mind doing that. . . . Please yourself then. . . . (*Upset again*) Not very good. I've only just got up. . . . Well yes, I think we should. Why don't you and Maureen come over here tonight? . . . I suppose we could all come to you but I thought we'd be more comfortable here—I've got my central-heating on. . . . I'll expect you around eight. You'll be picking Maureen up, won't you? . . . See you both later then. (*She hangs up and re-dials immediately*)

Josey Who are you ringing?

Miriam I'm checking her line. She says it's out of order. She must think I'm stupid. I know exactly what she's done. She's walked all the way down the street to reverse the charges from a call box. It's ringing. (*She suddenly throws the receiver back on to the telephone*)

Josey What's the matter?
Miriam It was an obscene call. It must have been Hugh.
Josey It couldn't have been an obscene call—you rang him. What did he say?
Miriam He didn't say anything. There was just all this heavy breathing.
Josey Uncle Hugh couldn't be obscene even if he tried. You probably rang him up in the middle of an asthmatic attack.
Miriam Well it proves one thing at least.
Josey What?
Miriam There's nothing at all wrong with their telephone.
Josey You could have got a wrong number.
Miriam Do you think so? Perhaps I ought to try again. (*She makes for the telephone*)
Josey On the other hand if you haven't, Uncle Hugh isn't going to like you very much—ringing him up when he's probably frantically looking for his pump.
Miriam Well it's not my fault. According to Margaret the telephone shouldn't be working. (*She dials again. When she gets an answer, she gestures to Josey to come and listen*)

Miriam hands the receiver to Josey and wanders upstage. Josey makes a passionate noise down the receiver and after a moment hangs up. She collects her things from the armchair

Josey See? Gone! All you've got to do is play them at their own game. (*She moves towards Miriam*)
Miriam Where did you learn to make noises like that?
Josey I lay awake in bed at night—and listen.

Miriam, for a split second, accepts the explanation, then realizes its implication. She points to the hallway and Josey makes a hasty retreat

All right, I'm going, I'm going.

Josey exits

Miriam Mucky little devil.

Slight pause. She takes out her father's letter from the pull-down flap out of the cabinet and sits on the settee. She ponders. We hear "Miriam's thoughts" (Miriam's voice pre-recorded)

Miriam's thoughts Go on, open it.
Miriam No, I can't.
Miriam's thoughts It's probably just a formality—you know what's in it.
Miriam If it's just a formality, what's the point of opening it?
Miriam's thoughts Well you have to be sure—just in case.
Miriam In case of what?
Miriam's thoughts He could have changed his mind. You'd look a right idiot in front of the others if he'd changed his mind. Best open it and be sure.

She is about to open it when another thought strikes her

I wonder if it's hereditary? Gaga.

She tosses the letter on to the seat next to her at the horrifying thought. Pause. She takes it up again. She opens it. She reads it hurriedly, the momentum becoming faster and faster as she reads on. She begins to laugh

Miriam (*speaking through her laughter*) I've got it . . . I've got it all.

Her laughter is quite hearty, and as it builds the front door slams. Suddenly her laughter turns to tears

Austin (*off*) You can stop that, it's only me.
Miriam (*sobbing*) I don't know who you think I am.

Austin enters, brushing himself down as it is now raining. He carries a newspaper

Austin (*as he enters*) I haven't been married to you for seventeen years and learned nothing. I know exactly what you are, Miriam.
Miriam I'm upset, that's what I am.
Austin You're a phoney. This is your husband. (*He sits in the armchair*) You don't have to put on a show for me. Save it for the others.
Miriam (*standing*) Well I've heard everything now. (*Advancing towards him*) Here I am, breaking my heart because I've just lost my father, and you've got the gall to call me . . . (*She snatches the newspaper from his hand*) And where have you been? The doctor said I shouldn't be left.
Austin The doctor's an idiot. I can see through you even if he can't.
Miriam (*rolling up the newspaper in temper*) I've had to suffer you calling me many things over the years, but to call your own wife a phoney at a time like this. (*She points at him with the rolled newspaper*) If my father was alive now——
Austin If your father was alive now he wouldn't be speaking to you. Just like he hasn't been for the last ten years. (*He snatches the newspaper back*)
Miriam We had our differences, I'll grant you that. But he mellowed towards the end.
Austin If you ask me he never forgave you for cremating your mother.
Miriam He had no-one to blame for that but himself.
Austin You knew he wanted her to be buried.
Miriam Well if he had been here and not in Chepstow *he* could have made all the funeral arrangements.
Austin They wouldn't let him out of intensive care. And if you hadn't bought him that deep-fat-fryer he wouldn't have been there in the first place.
Miriam Yes, go on, blame me for it.
Austin You can say what you like—he'd have been better off with an electric kettle.
Miriam It's easy to say that in retrospect. (*She ambles to the settee, picks up the letter, and sits*) At least it's comforting to know he forgave me in the end.
Austin How do you know he did?

She waves the letter

What's that?
Miriam A letter. He's left everything for me.
Austin Can I see?

Miriam nods. Austin goes and sits next to her. She hands him the letter and envelope

You've read the front of the envelope? It says: "To Miriam. To be opened in the presence of Maureen and Margaret".
Miriam I had to open it—just to be sure. He told me a couple of weeks ago that everything was to come to me. He could have changed his mind. I didn't want to look a fool in front of the others. I had to check he wasn't rambling.
Austin (*still reading the letter*) I didn't think you'd get the lot. In fact I'm surprised you got anything at all.
Miriam I knew he wouldn't forget me.
Austin What about the others?
Miriam Well they're bound to feel put out.
Austin Left out.
Miriam I'll take them out for a nice meal. (*She rises and makes for the cabinet*) You'll learn to accept a lot on a full stomach.
Austin That must be why you're such a good cook.

Miriam stops in her tracks, throws him a look, then continues to pour herself a drink

I still find it surprising there's no mention of Mavis.
Miriam He didn't have to worry about her. She's quite well looked after where she is.
Austin It's still a bit odd.
Miriam Of course she is. I don't suppose she'll ever come out of there.
Austin I wasn't talking about Mavis.
Miriam (*turning towards him*) And you still haven't told me where you've been.
Austin I've been to the hospital. They rang about an hour ago.
Miriam What for? (*Panicking*) My God, they haven't made a mistake?
Austin They wanted someone to identify the body.
Miriam (*relieved*) Thank heavens for that. You know for one horrible moment I thought ... why do you have to identify the body?
Austin I don't know. It's customary.
Miriam How's he looking? Does he look, you know—ill?
Austin Of course he looks ill—he's dead.
Miriam Sometimes they look different. What expression is he wearing?
Austin What expression would you like him to wear? Happy? Sad? Constipated? Let me know and I'll have a word with the undertaker. He just looks dead.
Miriam He must look something else as well.
Austin (*after thinking about it*) I suppose he looks sort of ... relieved.
Miriam (*shouting*) He's not supposed to look relieved. When the others ask how he looks I can hardly say "relieved".

Austin Why not? He probably is.

Miriam Perhaps it's best if the girls don't see him.

Austin They might want a last look.

Miriam Well *I* don't. I'd rather remember him as he was.

Austin Gaga.

Miriam The trouble with you is you've got no feeling.

Austin I've been numbed over the years.

Miriam All your family are the same. Hearts like granite.

Austin At least they're honest. They won't put a show on for anyone.

Miriam (*putting down her drink and taking out her hanky*) It comes to
  something when you can't get upset over the death of your own father.
  (*She attempts to cry*)

Austin Don't misunderstand me. I'd be quite touched to see you show some
  genuine emotion; but you're just not capable of it.

Miriam You say some terrible things.

Austin You never thought much of him when he was alive—and everybody
  knew it. Why bother to try and convince people otherwise now?

Miriam I suppose you'd rather me not shed a tear?

Austin Better that than glycerine.

Miriam Ooooh, I give up trying to get through to you.

There is a knock on the front door

  Austin goes to answer it

*Miriam takes the letter and envelope from the settee and returns it to the
cabinet, puts the remains of her glass of sherry back with the drinks in the
cabinet and goes and sits on the settee, with her hanky poised to her nose, ready
for whoever might be calling*

  *Austin enters and stands behind Miriam. He puts his hands on her shoulders
  and leans towards her*

Austin Tudor has come to see you, Miriam.

  Tudor enters. He is wearing wellingtons, raincoat and hat

Miriam (*panicking; without seeing Tudor*) No, I don't want to see him. Tell
  him I'm not here—tell him I'm not ... (*At this point she sees Tudor.
  Immediately, she puts on her "upset" act*) Hello, Tudor. How are you?

Tudor Come to offer my condolences, I have. (*Slight pause*) I know he'd
  been bad but it still come as a shock see, didn't it?

There is an awkward pause. Austin breaks it

Austin Sit down.

Miriam throws Austin a terrible look. Tudor sits in the armchair. Pause

Tudor How are the—er—rest of the girls?

Miriam (*still upset*) Maureen was awful when they told her. Margaret was
  upset, I suppose, but she still went to Tesco's shopping.

Austin Well they've got to eat.

Miriam I hope nothing happens to me on a Tuesday, because if it did, you'd still go to your ballroom dancing.
Tudor How did Mavis take it?
Miriam She hasn't been told yet.
Tudor Ah, I bet she'll be awful.

There is another pause

Miriam Well thanks for coming, Tudor. I'll tell the girls you've called.
Tudor I'm not going yet.
Miriam Oh, sorry. I thought perhaps you couldn't stay long.
Tudor No. No. (*Slight pause*) Avril was going to come with me but she's having a bit of trouble with her coil.
Miriam Pardon?
Tudor She's convinced it's the dynamo but I've told her it's the coil, it is. Well either that or she needs a complete re-bore. She's taken the car straight over to the garage. She's coming to the funeral though. She said, she wouldn't miss that for nothing—big end or no. (*He laughs heartily at his joke but stops abruptly when he realizes that no-one else has joined him. After a pause, tentatively*) What time is the—er—funeral?

Miriam resumes her crying

Austin Well it hasn't been——
Tudor Too early yet of course, ay ay, yes that's right. (*He looks at Miriam who is still crying then looks to Austin. He mimes for him to make Miriam a cup of tea*)
Austin (*bending over her left shoulder*) Tea, Miriam?
Miriam (*determinedly*) No thank you.
Tudor (*almost overlapping*) Two sugars for me and a lot of milk.

Austin exits to the kitchen

Pause

Tudor I don't want to speak ill of the dead, Miriam, but he'd been bad for a long time mind, hadn't he? (*He rises and moves towards her*) And it's pointless saying "Don't get upset" because I mean you will anyway, won't you? And I can say that now, see, without any fear of contradiction because I know how I felt when I lost my father. And the thing is, see, Miriam, he was no spring chicken now, was he? What, seventy-three, seventy-four?

Miriam nods

And we've all got to go sometime. And with *my* father it was a blessing in the end because, well, he was incontinent.
Miriam My father was that as well.
Tudor And why not, after all they were brothers.
Austin (*off*) Will you take Carnation, Tudor?
Tudor (*calling back*) A spray of chrysanths I thought of having.
Austin (*off*) Milk, I'm on about. Carnation milk.
Tudor Oh ay, yes, anything will do.

Tudor laughs at his misunderstanding but Miriam doesn't share his humour.
He goes and sits in the armchair. Pause

Only Aunty Cassie from Brixton left now see, isn't there?
Miriam Don't be silly, Tudor, she's dead and buried.
Tudor No she's not, don't be soft.
Miriam I'm telling you.
Tudor I wrote to her last month.
Miriam I sent her a wreath two years ago.
Tudor (*after a slight pause*) Well if she *is* dead, Miriam, I don't know who
the hell I've been writing to.
Miriam You'd better get in touch and tell her my father's gone. We'll just
have to wait and see who turns up.
Tudor What if she *is* dead?
Miriam Well then she won't turn up. And in any case I wouldn't worry
about it. The very worse that can happen is that I've got a medium for a
cousin.
Tudor You don't think I'm a medium, do you?
Miriam Well I don't know. I've always said there's a bit of Mavis about
you.
Tudor Mavis?
Miriam Rare, Tudor. Medium rare.
Tudor (*after a slight pause*) Well I didn't know Mavis was a medium.

Miriam shakes her head, trying to control her impatience. Pause

(*Tentatively*) There will be—er—flowers, will there?
Miriam We don't know yet. I imagine so.
Tudor (*rising and moving towards her slightly*) Only when your mother died,
there were no flowers—I sent a big bouquet and everybody thought I was
an idiot for not knowing. (*Wandering around*) And at Uncle Eddie's
funeral there were flowers, and no-one spoke to me because I didn't send
any. Well since then I like to get things straight as soon as possible. (*After
a slight pause*) So there's no flowers then?
Miriam (*almost ready to blow*) Tudor, I said I expect so. I'll let you know.
Tudor (*going and sitting next to her*) Ay, but how?
Miriam I'll give you a ring.
Tudor I'm not on the phone.
Miriam Then I'll get Austin to drop round and see you.
Tudor Well if I'm not there—if he can't get an answer—tell him to write it
down on a little piece of paper, and slip it in under the door.
Miriam (*after a pause*) Isn't Avril back from the garage yet?
Tudor I don't know. (*He stands*) Why then, do you want me to fetch her for
you?
Miriam (*panicking*) No! No I just thought you might have to be getting
back to her, that's all.
Tudor (*sitting down*) No no. She'll probably come over before the funeral
though. If it's only to see Mavis.
Miriam Mavis isn't coming here. She's going to Margaret's.

Tudor Is that right? Ooh, I bet she'll be disappointed.

Miriam She'll be livid.

Tudor And how will Margaret feel?

Miriam (*looking at him*) Livid.

Tudor (*after a pause*) Mavis came *here* the last time she was home didn't she?

Miriam (*rising*) I had her, yes.

Tudor How long ago is that, now then?

Miriam (*wandering downstage*) When did I have my nervous breakdown?

Tudor (*thinking about it for the briefest of moments*) Ooh, fifteen years ago.

Miriam Well it was fifteen years ago then.

Tudor So she hasn't been out in that time? What I mean is, you girls haven't seen her in fifteen years?

Miriam No. She broke out eighteen months ago. (*Turning to face Tudor*) Only got as far as the main gate—doubled back. Forgot where she was going.

Tudor There's no possibility of her coming out for good then?

Miriam She could come out tomorrow if there was someone to have her.

Tudor That's what I mean, there's no possibility of her coming out for good then. Couldn't you girls, you know, you sisters get together and sort something out?

Miriam (*shouting towards the kitchen*) Austin, hurry up with Tudor's tea.

Austin enters with a cup of tea

Austin (*handing tea to Tudor*) Here you are.

Miriam sits in the armchair

Tudor Thank you very much. (*Slight pause*) Miriam was just saying about Mavis, Austin.

Austin Oh yes.

Tudor Must be awful to spend all those years in a place like that.

Miriam She's happy enough.

Tudor Ay, but the thing is though, the thing is, Miriam, if you haven't seen her for fifteen years, how do you know?

Miriam Maureen went to see her a couple of weeks ago.

Tudor (*surprised to hear it*) Did she? How's she getting on?

Miriam Lovely. Tea too hot for you? Have more Carnation. Austin, use the one from the fridge.

Austin exits to the kitchen

Pause

Tudor Nasty day. (*After a slight pause*) Glad I put the wellies on. (*He attempts to laugh but cuts it short*)

Austin enters from the kitchen, pours Carnation milk in Tudor's tea and returns to the kitchen

Miriam It's raining so bad, Tudor, perhaps it would have been a good idea if you'd stayed in the house altogether.

Tudor I had to pay my respects.

Miriam You could have sent a card, I'd have understood.

Tudor It's not the same though, is it? And the thing is, Miriam, (*he checks over his shoulder that no-one is listening*) the thing is—between you and me—it'll take a lot more than a drop of rain to keep *me* in. (*He bursts into hysterical laughter*)

Miriam is dead-pan

Austin enters from the kitchen

Tudor directs his laughter towards Austin but he doesn't laugh, he doesn't know what's been said. Tudor tries to involve Austin once more in his joke. When Tudor realizes that neither Austin nor Miriam is going to join in with him, his laughter peters out. There is a pause

Would you like us to do anything?

Miriam (*after a slight pause*) Who?

Tudor Me and Avril.

Miriam When?

Tudor You know. On the day.

Miriam What day?

Tudor Well, the day of the (*miming the word*) funeral.

Miriam No, I think we'll be all right.

Tudor Will you want any help with the spread?

Miriam No thank you.

Tudor Avril is marvellous with the old sandwiches, mind. And I make a very good almond cake.

Miriam I'm sure we'll be able to manage.

Tudor Well, if you run short of anything, or you need a hand, just you give one of us a shout. One of us will come over.

Tudor sips his tea. It tastes pretty bad now with all that Carnation. He tries to hide it. He looks from Austin to Miriam, neither of them are looking at him. He takes the opportunity to put the cup down on the settee arm and make a hasty retreat

Well, I'm off now then. (*He stands*)

Austin and Mirian immediately stand and rush to him

Miriam Going?

Tudor Think I'd better make a move.

Miriam (*taking the risk of sounding disappointed*) Ooh, and you've only just come.

Tudor Thought perhaps I'd nip over and see Maureen. Offer my——

Miriam ⎫
⎬ (*together*) Condolences.
Austin ⎭

Tudor Yes.

Miriam I don't think she'll be there, Tudor. She had to go to the hospital on business. Identify the body and so on.

Austin looks at her in amazement

Why don't you go round to our Margaret's. I'm sure she'd love to see you.

Tudor (*uncomfortable about the idea*) Ahh, well the thing is, see, I've never felt as though Margaret has ever really liked me.

Miriam Nonsense, Tudor. She thinks the world of you.

Tudor (*beaming*) Does she?

Miriam Only yesterday she was asking about you.

Tudor Oh well, I'll nip over there then.

Miriam You'll be more than welcome with Margaret, Tudor. And I know for a fact *she's* got plenty of fresh milk.

Tudor I'll see you then.

Miriam Austin will let you know the day of the funeral.

Tudor You'll see me before then. When I bring Avril over.

Miriam (*pretending to have forgotten*) Oh yes, of course, I forgot. Tell me when you're coming as I can be sure to be in. (*Turning and moving away*) I'd hate to miss you both. (*Her expression says different*)

Tudor Shall we make it Tuesday?

Miriam (*turning towards him*) Lovely. What time?

Tudor Two o'clock?

Miriam Perfect. Austin will see you out. (*Putting on her act again*) You don't mind, do you? Only I don't feel up to it.

Tudor (*going to her*) I understand. I know exactly how you feel.

He puts his hands around her shoulders and gives her a big wet kiss on the cheek. After releasing her he turns to Austin and gives him a look which says: "poor thing"

Tudor turns and exits. Austin follows him out

Miriam waits for the door to slam and when it does she lets out one almighty scream and rushes to the cabinet

Austin enters

Miriam Where are those tablets the doctor left me. I want to take them. I want to take them all.

Austin Tudor's all right.

Miriam He's not your relation.

Austin (*sitting in the armchair*) True. And it's not as if you're short of a couple of Tudors in your family, is it? I reckon your grandmother and grandfather must have been brother and sister or something. There's definitely something wrong with the strain somewhere.

Miriam (*giving up looking for the tablets and turning to Austin*) You're in no position to criticize any of *my* family. Just take a look at your own.

Austin No-one has seen snow (*he points to the side of his head*) on my side.

Miriam You're forgetting Mansel.

Austin (*a sore subject*) He's not family.

Miriam You go as cousins.

Austin My grandmother reared him up that's all.

Miriam (*sitting on the settee*) I don't know about seeing snow, I reckon he must have been born in a blizzard.

Austin He only suffers with his nerves.

Miriam *I* suffer with my nerves.

Austin And I just suffer.

Miriam There's a difference in bad nerves and Mansel. If anyone ought to be put away, it's him.

Austin You can't put someone away just because he pulls a shopping trolley everywhere with him.

Miriam I know. It's the fact he keeps calling it Rover I'm on about.

Austin He's lonely. He had a dog and it died, that's what that's all about.

Miriam He's still got it I suppose? The trolley.

Austin As far as I know.

Miriam I wonder what he keeps in it.

Austin It's rumoured it's his life savings.

Miriam (*shaking her head*) I reckon it's about twenty tins of Pedigree Chum.

Austin He's never done anyone any harm.

Miriam Neither has Mavis.

Austin Come off it. Why do you think she's where she is? They don't call her Lizzy Borden for nothing.

Miriam That's not true. Mavis never hurt a fly.

Austin No, she just eats them. I'm telling you, I wouldn't like to be left in the same room as her.

Miriam She's never been violent.

Austin What about your eighteenth birthday?

Miriam She had a turn, that's all.

Austin A turn? She nearly killed me. And all I did was sit in her chair.

Miriam That was a long time ago.

Austin We've still got the chair, still got Mavis, and I've still got the scar.

There is a pause in which they each pout

Miriam No doubt I'll be the one allocated to break the news to Mavis.

Austin I can't understand why. It isn't as though you're renowned for your subtlety and tact.

Miriam Margaret won't want to do it that's for sure.

Austin Maureen will tell her if you ask her to.

Miriam Maureen will be too upset. No, that looks as though it's going to be another little job for Miriam.

Austin You shouldn't complain. Especially if everything *does* go to you.

Miriam What do you mean "if"? You've read the letter. You've seen it for yourself.

Austin But something doesn't smell right about it somehow.

Miriam What do you mean?

Austin Well for a start, I think it very odd that you have it all.

Miriam is about to speak but Austin continues

Think about it. Just think about the relationship you had with him over the years. If the shoe was on the other foot, would you have left it all to him?

Miriam thinks about it. Then she rises and wanders downstage

He's been up to something, take it from me. It wouldn't surprise me if he's left it to some cats' home. Or to some vagrant he met last year. It would be just like him to do something odd like that.

Miriam (*annoyed*) I've told you before, Austin. Apart from Mavis, and with the exception of Tudor, there is nothing at all odd about my family.

The telephone rings. Miriam looks at it before going to it. She picks up the receiver, breathes down it heavily several times, then replaces it. Austin can't believe his eyes. She looks at him. Black-out

CURTAIN

SCENE 2

The same. Later that evening

As the CURTAIN *rises, Miriam is placing a framed photograph of her father on the stereo unit. She stands back to look at it. Not happy with it there she takes it and places it on the coffee-table*

Austin enters. He is doing up his cuff-links

Austin (*moving to Miriam*) What are you doing?
Miriam It's a photograph of my father. I found it upstairs.
Austin You didn't lose it in order to find it. You put it up the attic ten years ago, when you and he fell out over that holiday business.
Miriam I thought I ought to put it out—under the circumstances.
Austin I don't see why. It isn't as if he's going to know anything about it.
Miriam The girls are coming over.
Austin Ah yes, of course.
Miriam Do you like it there?
Austin (*standing back in order to get a better view of it*) I think I preferred it up the attic.
Miriam (*moving it to another angle*) I won't keep it out of course. After the funeral it can go back up the loft.
Austin Not to sustain any memories.
Miriam That's right.
Austin You're all heart, Miriam. (*After a slight pause*) Are you sure I've got to go out tonight?
Miriam Absolutely. (*Moving to the cabinet*) We girls have things to discuss. I don't want you hanging round.
Austin Perhaps I can be of some help. Arbitrator. (*He sits in the armchair*)
Miriam (*turning towards him*) If you think this meeting is going to be some sort of slanging match I'm afraid you're going to be very much mistaken. I would'nt suggest for one minute that we girls are extremely close, but we are all civilized people. We do have feelings.
Austin Well one of you does.

Miriam Thank you, Austin. That's the first kind word you've said to me today.

Austin I meant Maureen.

Miriam (*returning to the cabinet and pouring herself a sherry*) Shouldn't you be going? I don't want you here when they arrive.

Austin Afraid I'll interefere with your performance? If I'd thought I could have borrowed Gerald's video equipment. It might be in the interest of history to keep this meeting on record. And then, in a couple of years or so, one night when there's nothing on the telly, you and I can sit down and watch for an hour what could be the rumblings of world war three.

There is a knock on the door

Miriam Look they're here.

Austin Shall I let them in, or you?

Miriam You do it. I'm in mourning.

Austin exits

Miriam puts away her glass of sherry and takes up her position downstage with her hanky poised to her nose

> *Margaret enters alone. She is not too wet as she's parked the car outside the front door*

Margaret (*entering and making straight for the armchair*) What a ghastly night. (*She doesn't sit but puts her clutch handbag down on the chair and bends down to get out her handkerchief*)

While she is doing this, Miriam whimpers, just loud enough to be heard. Margaret stops and looks in Miriam's direction. They both look at each other. There is a brief moment before they fake their tears of bereavement and rush together to embrace each other c

Miriam (*in mid-flow of Margaret's tears*) Let me take your coat. (*She slips it off Margaret's shoulders*)

> *Miriam exits to the hall*

Margaret sits in the armchair

(*Off*) Where's Maureen?

Margaret I arranged to meet her at the bus stop. I waited for two minutes — she didn't turn up.

Miriam enters

Miriam (*going to Margaret*) You might have picked her up at the house seeing as it's such a lousy night.

Margaret All the way up there. That would have taken at least half a gallon of petrol. And besides, she lives in a cul-de-sac and I can never find reverse. She'll probably hop on a bus.

Miriam Would you like a drink? Sherry? Gin?

Margaret I'll have a Tia Maria and lemonade.

Miriam Sherry or gin.
Margaret (*after a slight pause*) Sherry.

Miriam goes to the cabinet and pours the sherry

Austin enters

Austin I'm off now then.
Miriam See you later.
Austin About what time?
Miriam We should be all done by ten.
Margaret She's not throwing you out, Austin?
Austin That I should be so lucky. (*He winks at Miriam*) Bye. Oh, and er—
break a leg.

Austin exits

Miriam takes the sherry to Margaret

Margaret Break a leg? What on earth does he mean?
Miriam Take no notice. It's just one of his little jokes. (*She returns to the cabinet to refill her own glass*)
Margaret This is all new, isn't it?
Miriam What?
Margaret The room.
Miriam We had it done a few weeks ago.
Margaret When you realized things were looking bad for Father.

They look at each other and both force a smile.

You were always very good at preparing, Miriam. Even as a child.
Miriam (*going and sitting on the settee*) I just like things to be organized.
Properly.

There is a pause while each take a sip of their drink. Margaret looks at Miriam and waits for her to look in her direction. When she has her attention, she speaks

Margaret It was very touching, you know. To be there at the end.
Miriam (*defending herself*) I would have been there too. But as you know I
was heavily involved in the Bring and Buy.
Margaret He asked where you were.
Miriam You didn't tell him?
Margaret Now would I?

She sniggers at Miriam and Miriam sniggers back

I said you were too upset to come.
Miriam That's right. There wasn't any need for him to know.
Margaret You misunderstand. He didn't *want* you there. He was just
checking you weren't in the room. He wanted to talk to me in private.
Miriam He didn't have enough breath to talk. What did he say?
Margaret I'm afraid I'm not able to tell you. It's something very personal
between Father and me. After all, I was his favourite.

Miriam almost chokes on her sherry

   Josey enters. She is dressed and ready to go out

Miriam I thought you'd gone out.

Josey Just going. You couldn't lend me a fiver, could you?

Miriam What have you done with your pocket money?

Josey Spent it.

Miriam Already? You only had it yesterday.

Josey Seven quid doesn't go very far.

Miriam You've spent seven pounds since yesterday?

Josey Well I went out last night, and I spent the rest this morning. (*Looking to Margaret, then to Miriam*) I bought a wreath.

Miriam This morning? You bought a wreath this morning?

Josey nods

   Your grandfather didn't die until this afternoon.

Josey I'm psychic.

Miriam You're a liar.

Josey All right I'm not psychic. Anyway, I didn't buy the wreath for Grandad. I bought it for a friend. He's being buried tomorrow.

Miriam It's Sunday tomorrow.

Josey Is it? Sorry, I meant Monday.

Miriam I don't know who you're following for lies. (*She slyly looks across at Margaret*)

Josey Are you going to lend it to me or not?

Miriam No.

Josey I'll just have to stay in then. (*She comes and sits on the settee*)

Miriam You can't we're having a meeting.

Josey I've got nowhere else to go. (*Slight pause*) Lend me some money, come on.

Miriam No, I said.

Josey The least you can do is lend me a fiver with all the money you got coming to you.

Miriam almost has a fit. Margaret has picked this up and is now taking far more interest in the conversation. Miriam rushes over to the cabinet to get her purse

Miriam I don't know if I've got any change. (*Looking in her purse*) I've only got a ten pound note.

Josey That'll do.

Miriam Can you change ten pounds, Margaret?

Margaret I didn't bring my purse with me.

Miriam Surprise surprise.

Margaret Pardon?

Miriam I found one behind my credit card.

Josey rushes up and snatches it out of Miriam's hand

Josey Thanks.

Josey runs out

Miriam (*calling after her*) And don't forget the date! (*She replaces her purse in the cabinet and crosses to Margaret*) More sherry?

Margaret drinks up and hands Miriam her glass. Miriam takes it and pours another sherry

Margaret (*after a pause*) I had a visitor this afternoon. Tudor!
Miriam (*covering a smile*) He called in here too.
Margaret He said.
Miriam I told him it would be pointless going to see you but he insisted. (*She almost laughs. She hands Margaret her sherry and then sits on the settee*) Stay long?
Margaret Three hours. I couldn't get rid of him. He kept going on about carnations and fresh milk.
Miriam (*after a slight pause*) Oh by the way, your telephone is working now.
Margaret Yes, the operator rang and said it was all fixed. Although Hugh isn't at all convinced. We keep getting crossed lines. Someone rang earlier, when he was having one of his turns. It was an obscene call.
Miriam (*uncomfortable*) There are some funny people about.

There is a pause

Margaret I hope she's not going to be late. Maureen.
Miriam Perhaps she's having trouble finding someone to sit with Rupert. Or maybe she missed the bus.
Margaret I can only stay until half-past nine. Rupert shouldn't be a problem, surely Desmond can stay in and watch him.
Miriam Desmond wouldn't stay in for anyone.
Margaret I suppose he still drinks?
Miriam More than ever.
Margaret She should never have married him. I did try to tell her at the time but she wouldn't listen to me.
Miriam Well you can hardly blame her—she was seven months pregnant.
Margaret That's not the point.
Miriam She took a chance. She wasn't to know how he would turn out.
Margaret I had a pretty good idea. I can tell a drinker from fifty yards. (*Leaning towards her and pointing with her glass of sherry*) I'll say this for Hugh, he's never touched a drink in all the years we've been married.
Miriam (*also leaning towards her*) Drink costs money, Margaret. And in all the years he's been married to you, you've never given him any.
Margaret I've always been thrifty, yes. But there's no harm in that. If I hadn't been that way I wouldn't have had the shop. And where would Hugh and I be today without that?
Miriam How is the baby business? (*She rises and pours herself another sherry*)
Margaret You make it sound as though I sell them.
Miriam Baby clothes then, you know what I mean.

Margaret No matter how tight money may be people will always get enough together to buy a pretty dress or romper.

Miriam Then it's a good thing we're not all as thrifty as you.

Margaret It wouldn't do for us all to be the same.

Miriam I'll drink to that.

They do. There is a long and angry knock at the front door

Margaret There she is.

> *Miriam exits to the hall*

Miriam (*off*) Come on in, you're drenched.

Maureen (*off, shouting*) Drenched? I'm soaking. Where is she, I'll bloody kill her. I can see she's here, I recognized the car.

Miriam (*off*) Now don't make a row.

Maureen (*off*) Make a row? I should have known better than to make arrangements with her.

> *Maureen storms in. She is soaked through to the skin. So too is her nine year old son, Rupert, who follows her in. Maureen is wearing a headscarf and a coat that is some sizes too small for her as she is eight and a half months pregnant. She is carrying a handbag and a pint of milk. Rupert is carrying a carrier bag which contains his Star Wars electronic game. Miriam comes in behind them*

(*To Margaret*) Where the hell were you?

Margaret (*quite emphatically*) I was there. I waited for ten minutes, I couldn't stay any longer.

Maureen What time did you get there?

Margaret Ten to eight.

Maureen (*shouting*) Couldn't have. I've been there since a quarter to.

Margaret (*insisting*) I was there, Maureen. I even went up the street. The house was all in darkness.

Maureen Well that's bloody funny because I left the front-room light on.

Margaret Perhaps I looked in the wrong house, then. It's such a long time since I've been there.

Maureen makes a face to Miriam at Margaret's bare-faced lie. She hands Miriam the pint of milk she is carrying

Rupert Mammy, I'm wet.

Miriam (*helping Maureen off with her coat*) I'll get some towels.

> *Miriam exits to the bathroom*

Rupert sits on the settee

Margaret Goodness, is that Rupert? Hasn't he grown?

Maureen (*sitting on the arm of the settee*) Yes, well he was only eighteen months old the last time you saw him.

Rupert begins to jump up and down on the settee. He doesn't have anything as comfortable as that at home

Margaret Doesn't time fly.

Maureen (*turning towards Rupert*) Say hello to your——(*She sees him jumping up and down and lashes out to slap him across the shoulders*) Behave. Say hello to your aunty Margaret, Rup. Take a good look at her 'cause you'll probably be twenty-one before you see her again. (*She takes out a cigarette and a box of matches from her handbag*)

Margaret Yes, we should keep in touch more.

Rupert Mam?

Margaret I must remember to put you on my Christmas card list.

Rupert Mam?

There is a pause in which Maureen gives Margaret a look

Mam?

Maureen lashes out at Rupert again

Maureen Now you know what I've told you. You've got to sit down there and be quiet.

Margaret Couldn't he have stayed with anyone?

Maureen (*firmly*) No. (*She lights her cigarette*)

Rupert Can I play with my Star Wars?

Maureen Wait till you get dry first.

Margaret I don't know who he looks like.

Maureen (*looking at Rupert*) His father.

Margaret Do you think so?

Maureen (*still looking at him*) They all look like him.

Margaret All?

Maureen (*turning to Margaret in an attempt to shock her*) All the kids in the street.

There is a pause. Margaret looks almost disgusted

Margaret (*in an attempt to lighten the situation*) I don't suppose I'd recognize Anthony or Samantha now.

Maureen (*dragging on her cigarette and facing out front*) Samantha married well and went to live in Bolton.

Margaret Yes, I remember. I was so disappointed not to be able to go to their wedding.

Maureen (*not looking at her*) I'm sure.

Margaret I trust they bought a nice gift with the cheque I gave them?

Maureen (*facing her*) Ay. They got an egg timer.

Miriam enters with two hand towels. She gives them to Maureen

Maureen (*handing a towel to Rupert*) Here! Wipe dry! (*She puts her cigarette down*)

Miriam pours Maureen a sherry. Maureen and Rupert put their towels over their heads and rubs vigourously

Margaret (*after a slight pause*) Hair-dryers are very good you know.

Maureen (*from under the towel*) I have got one but I didn't think to bring it with me. Aren't I silly?

Margaret I don't know what I'd do without mine. It's a very expensive one. It has all different types of attachments. I swear by it.

Maureen (*still from under the towel*) Well if it's got that many attachments it's no wonder you haven't got any *kids*. (*She physically laughs from under the towel*)

Miriam (*handing Maureen a sherry*) Here's a sherry for you, Maureen.

Maureen (*putting the towel around her neck*) Oh, ta. I brought some milk to have some coffee.

Miriam (*returning to the cabinet*) Yes all right, later on.

Rupert Am I dry now?

Maureen (*feeling his head*) Ay, you'll do.

Rupert Can I play with my Star Wars now?

Maureen Pass me that fag first.

Rupert does so. Then he takes out his Star Wars electronic game and sits on the floor in front of the settee with his back against the arm

Nice drop of sherry.

Margaret Yes, it's dry isn't it?

Miriam That's right.

Margaret I prefer a sweet myself.

Maureen Oooh Rupert's got a sweet. Offer your aunty a fruit pastille, Rup.

Rupert stands and struggles to get the packet from out of his trouser pocket. Margaret laughs hysterically at Maureen's misunderstanding

Margaret I was referring to the sherry. I meant I prefer sweet as opposed to dry. (*She still laughs*)

Maureen (*annoyed*) All right. You should have made yourself a bit more clear.

Rupert goes to Margaret and offers her a sweet. She smiles at the boy. She is at odds as to whether she should take one or not

Margaret Thank you very much.

As she reaches out to take one of the sweets, Rupert takes one out for her and hands it to her. She doesn't really want it now but takes it from him. She holds it in her hand not knowing quite what to do with it. She becomes aware of the others watching her. She puts it down on the table

I'll keep it for later.

Rupert goes to Miriam and offers her one

Miriam No thank you, sweetheart.

Margaret watches him as he returns to his game

Margaret Aren't you going to offer your mother?

Rupert She don't like them.

Margaret Well she has certainly changed. She used to steal all mine when we were children.

Maureen I find it very hard to believe you were ever a child, Margaret. It seems to me that you've been forty ever since you were ten.

Miriam (*sitting on the settee*) How old are you?

Margaret I've stopped counting.

Maureen (*to Miriam*) She's thirty-eight.

Margaret I'm no such thing.

Maureen Yes you are.

Margaret I'll be thirty-six next birthday.

Maureen Like hell you will. You're eleven months older than me.

Miriam I'm thirty-six.

Maureen (*to Miriam*) That's right. (*To Margaret*) And you're not twins.

Margaret You've both got it all wrong. I know exactly how old I am. (*She takes out a calculator from her bag and starts tapping away*)

Maureen (*to Miriam*) Look at her. (*To Margaret*) You can tap on that for as long as you like, love. You'll be thirty-nine next March.

Miriam Another sherry?

Maureen hands the glass to Miriam who returns to the cabinet

Margaret According to this I'm fifteen. I must have pressed the wrong button.

Maureen Either that or your batteries are flat.

Margaret Could be.

Miriam How long have you had the calculator?

Maureen (*over her shoulder to Miriam*) Ever since she got rid of the beads.

Maureen and Miriam laugh

Margaret There's something wrong somewhere. I'm fifty-three now.

Miriam hands Maureen her sherry

Maureen Oh put it away, and go and look for your birth-certificate when you get home.

Miriam Another sherry, Margaret?

Margaret (*putting the calculator back in her bag*) I'd better not—I'm driving.

There is a slight pause. During the following, Rupert becomes bored with his Star Wars game and returns it to the carrier bag. He wanders round the room

Miriam Right. Shall we start then? I don't want to go on too late, I've had a harrowing day and I'd like an early night.

Maureen (*interrupting*) Hey, what about me then?

Miriam (*interrupting*) Not that I'll sleep of course. I'm far too upset for that.

Maureen Now don't you start. (*Pointing her thumb towards Margaret*) It's bad enough I've got to put up with her.

Pause

Well where *are* we going to start?

There is no reply

Well is there going to be any flowers?

Margaret (*quickly*) Well *I* don't think there should.

Maureen Why not?

Miriam (*advancing towards Margaret*) Because you won't get a spray under six pounds, that's it, isn't it?

Margaret Don't be ridiculous.

Miriam (*to Maureen*) I knew we'd have this trouble with her.

Margaret Our father liked flowers to be in the garden.

Maureen ⎫ (*together*) Who said?
Miriam ⎭

Margaret He said.

Miriam When?

Margaret He didn't want flowers. He told me. With his dying breath. "I don't want flowers," he said.

Maureen Right. No flowers.

Miriam How do we know she's telling the truth?

Maureen We don't.

Margaret I wouldn't lie about something like that.

Miriam You'd lie about anything if you thought it would save you a couple of pounds.

Maureen (*shouting to shut them up and perhaps prevent a developing row*) Next! The undertaker. Who are we going to have?

Miriam V. M. Owen. The same one who buried our mother.

Margaret Our mother wasn't buried. None of us are likely to forget that.

Miriam turns away from Margaret

Maureen Are there any objections to him?

There is no reply from either of them

V. M. Owen it is then. What about the vicar?

Margaret The one who kept visiting him in hospital was nice.

Maureen Who is he?

Miriam He's not a proper vicar. He only does it part time.

Maureen Can he bury people?

Margaret He married Hugh's nephew.

Maureen Well he must be all right. He'll do. We'll have him. What's his name?

Margaret I don't know. I'll find out.

Maureen Good. Now the funeral. When shall we have it?

Margaret How about Thursday?

Maureen Why Thursday?

Miriam It's obvious, isn't it? Half-day early closing.

Margaret It's not that at all. But . . . if it was any other day, I would have to find someone to cover me in the shop.

Maureen Aren't you going to shut it?

Margaret (*amazed*) Shut the shop?

Maureen As a mark of respect.

Margaret But it's our livelihood.

Miriam (*facing Margaret*) I'm sure you're not going to starve if you close it for twenty-four hours.

Margaret What will Hugh say?

Miriam He won't say anything. You make all the decisions.

Margaret I don't see anything wrong with Thursday if the rest of the week is of no difference to you.

Maureen Right. Thursday it is then. Now what's next?

Miriam The service. Where is it going to take place?

Margaret The chapel of rest, surely.

Miriam (*determined*) He's not going from that place.

Margaret Why ever not?

Miriam Because he didn't want to go from there.

Margaret How do you know?

Miriam He told me. With his dying breath he whispered it to me.

Maureen Seems to me he said a hell of a lot with his dying breath.

Miriam (*insisting*) "I want to go from the house", he said.

Maureen Then from the house it will be.

Margaret Whose house?

Maureen His own.

Miriam You can't let him go from his own house. It's not right.

Maureen Why not?

Miriam (*making a face at Maureen*) Because you can't leave a corpse on its own. (*Nudging Maureen on the shoulder*) He can't go from his own house. He'll have to go from someone else's.

Maureen Whose?

Miriam (*facing Maureen, but pointing towards Margaret with her thumb*) Hers!

Margaret (*emphatically*) He can't go from my house.

Miriam (*facing her*) Why not?

Margaret Well it's er . . . (*A little lost for words*) It's Hugh . . . and his chest. All that pollen will go straight to his chest. And he's got hayfever too.

Miriam There's no flowers, remember?

Margaret (*frantically trying to think of another reason*) I don't have room. The only place I've got is the garage.

Miriam That'll do.

Margaret Don't be ridiculous. We can't put him out there.

Maureen I'd have him with me but there's scaffolding everywhere in my house.

Miriam He'll be all right in the garage. We can bring him in for the service.

Margaret Why can't you have him here?

Miriam Now where would I put a coffin?

Margaret The same place as I would.

Miriam But I haven't got a garage.

Margaret Well he's my father and I won't have him kept in a place like that. And besides, where would I put my car in this weather?

In disgust, Miriam goes to the cabinet and has another glass of sherry

Maureen What if we put him in his own house and we girls slept over there in turns.

Margaret I'm not sleeping in any house with a corpse.

Miriam But he's your father.

Margaret I don't care who he is.

Maureen Well I can't think where else to put him.

Margaret (*to Miriam*) Put him in your front room.

Miriam And where would you suggest I put my walnut cabinet, piano and room-divider?

Maureen I've got an idea. Why don't we leave him in the chapel of rest till——

Miriam I won't have him going from——

Maureen (*shouting*) Listen for a minute, will you? Why don't we leave him in the chapel of rest till the service, but we won't have the service there, we'll have it in one of the houses. The coffin can stay outside with the hearse.

Miriam Well I've only got one thing to say about that.

Margaret Who's house?

Miriam Exactly.

Maureen Which one of you two are going to give in?

Margaret I'm not.

Miriam (*sitting on the settee*) Neither am I.

Maureen looks from one to the other. A complete stale-mate. Maureen can't think of what to suggest next. Suddenly she has a thought

Maureen Shall we toss a coin?

Miriam (*seething indicating Margaret*) Everything that has happened to this family *she's* got out of.

Maureen (*to Miriam*) Will you agree to that?

Miriam looks away

Margaret?

Margaret I'll take a chance, yes.

Maureen Is it all right with you, Miriam?

Miriam It looks as if it will have to be, doesn't it? Have you got a coin?

Maureen (*looking in her bag for her purse*) I don't know. (*Directing her next remark towards Margaret*) I think I spent all mine on the bus.

Whilst Maureen searches for her purse and no-one is looking, Rupert takes a bite from one of the apples in the fruit bowl and then returns it without being spotted

Miriam Well, it's pointless asking her. She's like the queen, she doesn't carry money around with her.

Maureen (*finding a ten pence piece*) Here we go then. (*She tosses it and then goes to Margaret*) Heads or tails?

Miriam (*standing*) Don't ask her. *I* want to call.

Maureen Is it all right, Margaret?

Margaret Yes, carry on.

Maureen (*moving to Miriam*) Heads or tails?

Miriam I've changed my mind. Let her call instead.

Maureen (*giving her a push*) Hey, come on for God's sake.
Miriam (*after a slight pause*) Heads.

Maureen takes her hand away from the coin to reveal it. She looks up at Miriam and then holds her hand out for Miriam to see

(*After seeing the coin*) Best of three!
Margaret (*protesting*) That's not fair.
Miriam It's what you would have said.
Margaret We should have agreed that at the beginning. You're nothing but a crook.
Maureen I'll toss again. (*She does. To Miriam*) Call.
Miriam She can do it this time.
Maureen (*under her breath*) Well, bloody hell. (*She crosses to Margaret. She waits for her to call*)
Margaret Heads.

Maureen reveals the coin again in the same way as she did it first. As Margaret sees the coin she giggles childishly at the fact that she has won. Maureen looks across at Miriam

Miriam (*storming towards them*) Just a minute—let me see that. (*She takes the coin from the back of Maureen's hand and inspects it closely. She realizes she has lost*) She's always been a lucky sod. (*She tosses the coin at Margaret and it lands on her lap. She marches away in a fury*)
Maureen So we do have the service here then.

Margaret has now picked up the ten pence piece and is about to put it in her bag on the floor beside her

Miriam Don't forget to have your ten pence back, Maureen. Two minutes and it'll be in her pocket.

Margaret immediately changes her mind and hands the money back to Maureen. Rupert is now sitting back to front on the actual corner display unit of the settee

Margaret I wish you'd stop painting me as a penny pincher.
Miriam Well I can't help it, you are. I've never known anyone like you.
Margaret I'm careful, that's all.
Miriam Careful? (*To Maureen*) Do you know, she's got a beautiful Christmas tree in the house, with a hundred and ten fairy-lights. She puts them on the tree every year but she won't plug them in. Same with the wall-lights.

Miriam picks up an apple and sees it has been bitten. She looks at Rupert who looks away. Grudgingly, she hands it to him

Maureen Shall we get back to the funeral?
Margaret There's no need to get nasty just because you lost the toss. The trouble with you, Miriam, is you were never a good loser.
Maureen We've settled the service. Now we come to the problem—of Mavis.

Miriam (*turning towards them; her engine still running*) Well that's easily solved. (*Pointing to Margaret*) She's having her.

Margaret I couldn't possibly. Not with the responsibility of the shop.

Miriam *I* had her last time.

Margaret I know you did and she enjoyed it very much. She told me.

Miriam Told you? She doesn't even speak to *you*.

Margaret Well that settles it then, doesn't it? There's no way she would want to come to me.

Maureen It does make it difficult if Mavis doesn't speak to her.

Miriam Doesn't speak to her? She doesn't even know her. She doesn't know me either for that matter.

Maureen Well no wonder, she hasn't seen you buggers for fifteen years.

Miriam Maybe that's why then. Mother always taught us not to talk to strangers.

Maureen Is it decided then? Is Mavis coming here?

Miriam (*exploding*) I'm *not* having Mavis *and* my father.

Maureen Shall *I* have her then?

Margaret Yes, why not.

Miriam You can't have her, Maureen. You're going to have a baby. She's going to have a baby any day.

Margaret What if we ask Mavis where she'd like to stay.

Miriam Oh yes, you can safely suggest that knowing full well she'd never choose you.

Margaret The only other alternative is to leave her where she is.

Maureen And not have her out for her own father's funeral?

Margaret Why not? It will come as a terrible shock for her to learn that her father has just died. She probably never knew she had one in the first place.

Miriam You can't do that. You can't leave her in there. This is a time when the whole family should be together.

Margaret I agree. Together in *your* house.

Maureen What if we only have her out for the day? She could go back in in the night.

Margaret That sounds reasonable.

Miriam Will *you* look after her?

Margaret I would of course. But the service is going to be held here. I imagine we'll be staying here for most of the day.

Miriam (*almost on the verge of tears*) She's done it again. She's got out of this one as well. (*Her temper gets the better of her*) Houdini's got nothing on her.

Maureen So Mavis *is* coming here then?

Miriam For the day. She's back in by seven.

Maureen Right. Now then—how are we going to do the spread?

Margaret (*rising*) Well for a start, it obviously has to take place here.

Miriam Obviously.

Margaret Well we can hardly have the service here and the tea and comfort somewhere else, Miriam.

Maureen (*after biting her fingernail*) How are we going to work it? (*She then spits it out from the end of her tongue*)

Miriam The three of us will have to chip in and pay for it between us.

Margaret We're four girls.

Miriam You can't expect Mavis to pay for anything.

Margaret I don't see why not. She'll probably eat it the same as everyone else.

Miriam (*determined to have her way over something*) It'll be the three of us, Margaret, and that's an end to it. Shall we make it a fiver each?

Margaret (*in amazement*) That's fifteen pounds! You could cater a whole wedding for that.

Miriam I'm sure you could, yes.

Maureen Listen, I may as well tell you. *I* haven't got a fiver.

Margaret There we are, you see? We'd better make it three.

Maureen I haven't got three pounds either, luv.

Margaret Wouldn't Desmond give you something?

Maureen Desmond? The only thing he ever gives me lately is babies.

Margaret What if we all brought something instead.

Maureen I can bring a big pork pie.

Margaret I'll bring the cheese and, (*to Miriam*) you can bring something to go in the sandwiches.

Miriam Sandwiches? What about the bread and butter? The tea and cake?

Margaret Maureen can bring the butter, you the bread and Tudor offered an almond cake.

Miriam Have you ever tasted Tudor's almond cake? (*She shakes her head*) I have. I only took one bite and there were three teeth in it. And when I looked they were mine.

Maureen We'll do that then, shall we?

There is no reply

Right. Now we come to Father's business. The house etc.

Miriam Well I'm afraid I must intervene here. (*She goes to the cabinet and takes out Father's letter*) You may or may not be aware of the fact, but Father and I had a very special relationship towards the end.

Margaret Yes that's right. You talked and he listened. What a way to go.

Miriam He spent many an hour confiding in me. Telling me how he really felt about things—(*meaning Margaret*) and people. It's true that for many years we never saw eye to eye, but it was a great comfort for him to know, before he went to his grave, that he was finally forgiven.

Margaret Who forgave him?

Miriam I did.

Margaret For what?

Miriam For the way he treated me in my youth. For all the harsh words he's spoken to me over the years. Yes, it was difficult for me to do, but forgiveness has never been an easy virtue. And it hasn't gone unrewarded. My father left me this. (*She holds up the letter*)

Margaret Is that all. He left me the house.

Maureen What house?

Margaret His house.

Maureen He can't have. He's left that to me.

Margaret ⎱ *(together)* ⎰ Now don't be silly, Maureen.
Maureen ⎰   ⎱ That house is mine. And it's not bloody silly, luv.

Miriam Just a moment, just a moment, please! He might have *told* you lots of things, but it's all written down here. (*She waves the letter*) Everything goes to me.

Maureen I've got one of those letters too.

Margaret So have I.

Miriam And it *says* it all comes to me.

Maureen And mine does.

Margaret Mine too.

There is a pause. Miriam has an idea

Miriam The date. Who has the latest letter.

Maureen and Margaret look at each other. After a second they both dive into their bags for the letter. They fish them out simultaneously

Maureen Mine's dated the fifteenth of September.

Margaret The fifteenth, yes, same here.

Miriam (*smugly*) Ah well, mine is dated (*she opens and looks at the letter*) the fifteenth of September.

There is a slight pause. Maureen starts to laugh

Maureen Ooohhh, the little bugger. (*She screws up the letter and tosses it over her shoulder. She laughs continually until her next line*)

Miriam I don't care what's written down, he told me I'm to have everything three weeks ago.

Margaret He told me I'm to have it all this afternoon.

Maureen laughs even louder at this

Miriam Why did he do it?

Margaret I'll tell you why. Because he was nothing but a sadistic, senile old sod, that's why.

Maureen suddenly stops laughing and springs to her feet

Maureen Hey, (*pointing her finger at Margaret*) don't you speak about my father like that.

Margaret (*dismissing her*) Oh sit down, Maureen, for goodness sake.

Maureen (*fuming and still pointing*) Say one word like that about my father again, and, pregnant or no, (*going for Margaret with all the venom she can muster*) I'll come over there and bop you one.

Miriam comes between them just in time to stop Maureen from laying Margaret out. She forces Maureen back to sit on the settee

Miriam Calm down, Maureen, for goodness sake calm down.

Maureen Well you'd better tell her to shut her mouth before I shut it for her.

There is a pause. Miriam adlibs in mime, calming Maureen down. Margaret, on the verge of tears, is quiet

Margaret He'd never been a father to me.
Miriam He might have stood a chance if you'd been a tidy daughter to him.

Maureen laughs again at this and sticks her tongue out at Margaret

Margaret I don't know what you're laughing, Maureen, he wasn't your father anyway.

Maureen stops laughing and looks stunned

Miriam Margaret!
Margaret Well it's about time she knew the truth. Tell her the real story, Miriam.
Maureen What story?
Margaret Our mother had you by someone else.

Maureen begins to cry hysterically and continues throughout the following

How do you think you're only eleven months older than me? Our father was never slow off the mark but he was never that quick.
Miriam If anyone was dropped off at the wrong doorstep it was *you*. (*To Maureen*) No-one ever treated you any different—except Margaret. She treated us both as if we were adopted.

Maureen cries even louder

(*To Margaret*) You ought to be boiled in oil.
Margaret Hark at you. You're only furious because you wanted to tell her first.

Maureen can't take anymore. She grabs Rupert by the arm and starts to race off with him

Miriam No, Maureen. Don't go.
Maureen (*hysterically, as she goes*) I am. I'm going. I'm not staying here no more and you can stick that pork pie right up your arse.

Maureen and Rupert exit

Slight pause

Miriam Well, you've done it now.
Margaret I only told her the truth. There's no harm in that.

Rupert comes back into the room

Miriam I don't object to Maureen knowing. It's the way you told her, and now wasn't the time.

Miriam and Margaret see Rupert. He looks from one to the other. Then he takes his carrier bag and his mother's handbag, which she left on the floor by the settee, turns to Margaret and pokes his tongue out at her

   Rupert rushes off

Margaret Well, I couldn't help it. I was furious and before I knew it, it was out of my mouth.

Miriam That's always been your trouble.

Margaret At least people know where they are with me. If they don't like me it's because I'm too straight.

   Tudor enters. He is followed by his wife Avril

Tudor Hello all. I won't stop, I can see you're both very upset. Only after leaving Margaret's this afternoon, I couldn't help thinking about what she had said.

Margaret What did I say?

Tudor (*to Miriam*) I knew it wouldn't be easy for you, not having a car, (*to Margaret*) and you not liking driving that much. We've just had ours back from the garage, so I said to Avril, "Come on", I said, "let's go get her for them". Bring her in, Avril.

   Avril exits to the hall

Miriam (*realizing*) Oh my God. It's Mavis!

   Mavis enters carrying a suitcase in one hand and dragging Avril in with the other

Tudor is beaming at his surprise. Miriam and Margaret just look astonished. Mavis sets her suitcase on the floor. She looks from Miriam to Margaret

Mavis (*very enthusiastically*) Well, I don't know who you are, but a merry Christmas to you all!

Black-out

Curtain

ACT II

The same. Thursday morning

When the CURTAIN *rises, Josey is looking for something in the pull-down flap section of the cabinet*

Austin enters, unheard by Josey

Austin Looking for something?

Josey frantically throws everything back and closes the pull-down flap immediately

Josey Er . . . yes. My Giro. Can't seem to find it.

Austin (*sitting*) I wonder why.

Josey (*indicating the pull-down flap*) I'm sure I saw it in there last.

Austin What day is it?

Josey Thursday, why?

Austin What day do you normally get your money?

Josey Friday.

Austin Well do you think that possibly has got something to do with it?

Josey (*embarrassed; laughing*) Of course, yeah. Funny. I've been thinking it's Friday all day.

Austin If it's your mother's letter from your grandfather you're after, it's upstairs in her bedside cabinet.

Josey Now why would I want that, Dad?

Austin Wouldn't you like just a little peek?

Josey I'm not bothered.

Austin Come off it.

Josey I'm not. Really. Not about *that* letter, any rate. It's the other one I'd like to have a look at.

Austin What other one?

Josey The one Mam brought home earlier on.

Austin I didn't know your mother'd been out.

Josey (*sitting on the settee*) Yeah. She went over to Gramps' house to sort a few things out and found a letter. A genuine one this time. I heard her trying to tell Mavis about it. I was sleeping in the chair. She was saying something about it was from the old man. That she'd found it in a biscuit tin amongst a load of old bills. It was addressed to Mavis. Mammy opened it and was getting in such a mess because Mavis wasn't under-standing any of it. Mammy wanted to take her upstairs to read her the

letter again, and Mavis thought she wanted to play hide and seek. I
started to laugh, Mammy realized I wasn't sleeping and threw me out of
the room.

Mavis enters. She carries her handbag

Mavis Hello. It's me again.
Austin (*attemping to get out of his chair*) I'm off.
Josey Don't be silly, she's not going to bite you.
Mavis (*holding out her hand*) My name is Mavis.
Josey (*shaking it*) Josey.
Austin She's only been here five days and that's the sixty-eighth time she's
introduced herself.
Mavis (*to Josey*) Do I know your friend?
Josey Austin this is Mavis. Mavis—Austin.
Mavis (*going to him and holding out her hand*) Pleased to meet you.
Austin (*with arms folded and turning away from her*) We've already met.
Mavis (*insisting*) How do you do.
Austin (*facing her*) It's me, Austin.
Mavis (*still holding out her hand*) Pleased to meet you.
Austin (*losing his temper*) It's me. Me!
Josey Shake hands with her—she'll be all right then.

Austin reluctantly shakes her hand

Mavis I'm Mavis.
Austin Ay, we know.
Mavis Who are you now then?
Austin (*exploding*) Austin!
Mavis (*shouting*) Austin! Yes, that's right. And Veronica.
Austin Who the hell is Veronica?
Josey (*laughing*) I think that's me.
Mavis I'm looking for my friend Sylvia. Have you seen her?
Josey Sorry, no.
Mavis Have you?
Austin Perhaps she's upstairs.
Mavis I'll go and look. (*She makes to go*)

*Austin and Josey look at each other and burst out laughing. Josey catches sight
of Mavis moving back towards Austin*

Josey Hey, Dad. Dad. Look.

*Austin looks at Josey and she makes eyes for him to look behind. When he does
he sees Mavis. He turns away immediately*

Mavis Pssst!

Austin takes no notice

  Pssst!

He still ignores her

Oi! (*She hits him on the arm with her handbag*) Do you like it here?
Austin Where?
Mavis Here, in this place.
Austin I live here.
Mavis Yes I know, but do you like it?
Austin I used to.
Mavis I don't. I'd rather have the other place. The people (*for the moment she means Josey*) are a bit funny here. (*She taps her head with her forefinger. She turns to leave*)

Miriam enters from the hall

There you are.
Miriam (*turning Mavis round by her arm*) Sit down. I want to talk to you. (*She brings her to the settee*) Shift, Josey.

Josey moves to the other end. Miriam sits Mavis down in the middle. For the moment, Miriam remains standing. Immediately Mavis sits down she springs to her feet again

Mavis (*holding out her hand*) My name's Mavis.
Miriam (*humouring her she shakes it*) How do you do. Would you like to take a seat?
Mavis (*doing so*) Thank you. Have we met before?
Miriam We had breakfast together this morning.
Mavis I thought you looked familiar. Have you met my new friends? That's Reggie, (*she indicates Austin*) and this is Angela. (*She indicates Josey*)
Miriam (*to Josey*) How do you do. (*To Austin*) How do you do.
Austin (*incredulously*) I'm beginning to wonder which one's Mavis.
Mavis (*immediately springing to her feet and advancing towards Austin the second she has heard her name*) Me! I'm Mavis. How do you do.

Miriam grabs Mavis by the arm and makes her sit down again. Miriam sits next to her this time

Miriam Josey, Austin, I want to talk to you. Now, as you are all aware, the death of my father has caused a small problem.
Austin What problem?
Miriam (*indicating Mavis with her thumb*) Her.
Mavis I'm no problem. My warden told me.
Miriam Shut up, Mavis.
Mavis She tells me that as well. (*She laughs to Josey*)
Austin She's no more of a problem now your father's gone.
Mavis (*shouting*) I'm going to tell my warden about you.
Miriam (*shouting back*) I am your warden.
Mavis Well tell her then.
Miriam Who?
Mavis You.

Miriam buries her face in her hands. Austin and Josey laugh together

Miriam (*pulling herself together*) Look, everyone. Now that my father is
dead, Mavis doesn't have anyone.
Austin She didn't have anyone when he was alive.
Mavis I got a sister.
Miriam You have three sisters.
Mavis No. Only one.
Miriam I'm your sister too.
Mavis I thought you were my warden. (*To Austin*) Hey, Ronnie, is the
warden my sister?
Miriam Ronnie?
Josey (*to Austin*) I think she's talking to you.
Austin Me?
Mavis Is Sylvia my sister?
Miriam Who is Sylvia?
Austin (*singing*) "What is she?"

*Austin and Josey laugh again. During the following, Mavis looks through her
handbag*

Miriam (*trying to bring some order into things*) I'll start again. I think it'll be
far easier and less confusing if I come straight to the point. I'm not having
her go back to that home.
Austin Well, that's fair enough. Who's going to have her?
Miriam We are.
Josey What?
Austin I can't live with that.
Miriam She's my sister, Austin. I've got to see that she's taken care of.
Austin She's been your sister for the last thirty-odd years. Her welfare has
never bothered you before.
Miriam Well no. But my father was alive then.
Austin Bullshit.
Miriam Pardon?
Austin Your father might have only just passed on, Miriam, but as far as
Mavis is concerned he's been dead for years. There's something going on
that you're not telling me about. Come on, Miriam, come clean.
Miriam Don't be silly. (*Through clenched teeth*) I'll explain later.
Josey Where will she sleep?
Miriam Don't worry, I won't ask you to give up your room. We'll put a bed
in the front room.
Austin I don't believe this.
Josey And where will you put the rest of the furniture?
Miriam I'll get rid of it.
Austin Including the walnut cabinet?
Miriam Including the walnut cabinet.
Josey It's amazing.
Miriam What is?
Josey You couldn't put a coffin in there, suddenly you've got room for a
double bed.
Miriam I didn't say anything about a double bed.

Austin What happened to, "Mavis is all right where she is, she's well taken
care of"?
Miriam She probably was. It's just that I'll sleep more comfortably
knowing she's safe here with me.
Austin I'll guarantee you won't sleep at all if she moves in here with us.
Miriam It'll be all right I tell you.
Austin Are you forgetting what it was like when she stayed the last time?
And that was only for a week. We were all on Valium—including the dog.
Mind you, she did keep the flies down.

*Just as Austin says his last line, Mavis pops a pill into her mouth, throws the
rest of the pills back into her bag and closes it immediately*

What's she doing?

Miriam looks at Mavis

Miriam (*to Austin*) What's the matter?
Austin She just took a tablet then.
Miriam (*to Mavis*) Did you?

Mavis looks at her questioningly

Have you got a tablet in your mouth?

Mavis shakes her head

Are you sure?

Mavis nods

Stick your tongue out.

Mavis doesn't

Go on, stick it out.

Mavis sticks her tongue out and leaves it so during the following

There's nothing on her tongue
Austin Then she's swallowed it. She did take something—I saw her.
Miriam (*turning to Mavis and seeing her with her tongue still out*) All right,
you can put it back now.

*Miriam has a thought. She looks at Mavis's handbag, then at Mavis. She
grabs the bag but Mavis won't let go. There is a struggle but Miriam wins.
Once she has got the bag from Mavis she stands up and opens it. She takes out
a strip of pills*

(*Unable to believe it*) She's on the pill!

Josey and Austin collapse with laughter again

Don't laugh, it's not funny. (*To Mavis*) Who gave you these tablets?
Mavis You did.
Miriam Me?
Josey She probably means the warden. You were the warden last.

Miriam Why do you take them, Mavis?
Mavis Well, so I won't have any babies.

Josey and Austin crack up again

Miriam (*to Austin, meaning Josey*) Get her out of here. Well I'm glad you can all laugh about it.

Mavis joins in the laughter, but immediately Miriam looks at her she stops

Did the warden give ... I mean did I give them to you?
Mavis Yes.
Miriam Did I have reason to?
Josey I would have thought so. I can't imagine them giving out the pill because they've run out of Smarties.
Miriam (*after a slight pause*) Do you have a boyfriend, Mavis?
Mavis Course I have.
Miriam Who is he? What's his name?
Mavis Burt.
Miriam Burt who? Get a pen, Austin, write this down.
Mavis Reynolds.
Miriam Burt Reyn——
Austin } (*together*) Burt Reynolds. (*Again they laugh*)
Josey }
Miriam She's having me on. Now look, Mavis. I want you to think before you answer the next question. It's very important to get it right.
Josey It could win you tonight's star prize—the new Austin Maestro.
Miriam Shut up, Josey. (*To Mavis*) Has anyone been taking advantage of you?
Austin Of course they haven't. Now she's on the pill *she* can take advantage of *them*.
Miriam Austin, we're going to have to ring that place. Heaven knows what's been going on there. Which brings me back to my point earlier on. She's not safe there anymore. She's far better off here with me.
Austin But how will we stay sane?
Mavis Yeah.
Miriam (*sitting down*) I'm not sure whether to take the pills from her now, or let her finish them off.

Mavis is counting on her fingers

Josey Oh I'd let her finish the month if I were you. You never know, she might have gone to an orgy last week.
Mavis Last Thursday.
Josey See?
Miriam What?
Mavis I haven't took them since last Thursday. I keep forgetting.
Miriam Would you like to give them to me, Mavis? I can see that you take one a day—every day—until you finish the course.
Austin You make it sound like penicillin.
Miriam Give them to me, Mavis.

Mavis No.

Josey Look, you're going about it all the wrong way. This is how to do it. Look, Mavis, you remember the warden (*pointing to Miriam*) giving you the pills? Well now she wants them back. You can still take them, but she'll give you one every day. Will you do that, Mavis? Will you?

There is a pause while Mavis looks at her. Then she waves two fingers at Josey rather quickly and laughs hysterically

Austin (*laughing*) So that's how you do it.

Miriam There's only one way to handle Mavis——

Austin And that's to leave her get on with it. Don't forget your eighteenth birthday party. I'd hate her to have another turn.

There is a knock on the front door

Josey I'll get it.

Josey exits

Miriam You're probably right. The last thing I want is to upset her.

Austin I don't know what you think you're doing. There's absolutely no possibility of her staying here for good.

Miriam You don't understand.

Austin I can't imagine what you're thinking of.

Miriam It's all to do with the letter.

Austin What letter?

Josey enters

Josey Visitors. (*She returns to her seat*)

Miriam (*to Austin*) I'll explain later.

Josey Tudor and Avril.

Miriam That's all I need.

Tudor and Avril enter

Tudor Hello all.

Miriam (*standing*) Tudor. Avril. There's nice to see you. (*It's not*) I'm sorry I can't offer you any tea. They're digging up a gas main at the bottom of the street so our cooker is off.

Tudor Funny. I didn't see any workmen about.

Miriam Which way did you come?

Tudor (*indicating with his finger*) The top way.

Avril (*indicating the same*) Top way.

Miriam Yes, well, they're at the bottom end. (*She heads for the cabinet*)

Mavis (*standing*) Hello. My name's Mavis.

Tudor Hello, luv.

Mavis Who are you then?

Tudor Tudor.

Mavis And who's this?

Tudor Don't you remember Avril?

Mavis Course I do. Sit down, Sandra.

Austin stands and gives Avril his seat

I'd better introduce you all. (*Introducing Josey*) This one's Jean.
Tudor (*nodding*) Jean.
Avril Jean.
Mavis And that's Arthur. (*She indicates Austin*)
Tudor (*saluting him*) Arthur.
Avril Arthur.
Miriam And this is the new one. (*Pointing to Miriam*) Dorothy.
Tudor (*smiling and nodding to Miriam*) Dorothy.
Avril Dorothy.
Mavis Only came in this morning. Attempted suicide. Tablets. (*Taking her pills from out of her bag*) Here you are, look. (*Giving them to him*) Keep them safe for her.
Miriam (*taking the pills from Tudor and gently pushing him out of the way*) Austin, why don't you take Mavis in the other room. Try the television, there might be something on for her—University Challenge, or Bagpuss.
Austin (*moving back to Miriam*) I'm not going in there on my own.
Miriam Josey will go with you.
Josey I was just going out. (*She gets up*)
Miriam You can go later. Come on, Mavis. Go next door with Doctor Davis and the nurse.

Mavis is now standing between Austin and Josey

Mavis Am I going to have an internal?
Miriam No, you're going to have your eyes tested.

   Austin and Josey carry Mavis off by her elbows

(*After a pause*) She's hard work, but she is my sister after all.
Tudor Of course, yes, exactly.
Avril Exactly.

Slight pause

Tudor Come about the arrangements I have. Austin never came round like you said he would.
Miriam Didn't he let you know? I told him to.
Tudor Had a lot on his mind I expect—with everything.
Avril Everything.
Miriam Well the service is today. It's from here. And it's one o'clock. (*She sits*)
Tudor Er—what about the spread, then?
Miriam What about it?
Tudor Will that take place here as well? Or is it going to be at someone else's?
Avril Else's?
Miriam No, that's here too. We were going to have it at my father's house but I thought better of it.

Avril stands up and tugs at Tudor's arm. They mouth something to each other

What is it?

Avril Go on, tell her.

Tudor (*after a slight pause*) Well, it's about Mavis. (*Wandering about*) We were talking about it the other night,.

Avril Night.

Tudor Weren't we?

Avril Yes.

Tudor Yes. And we thought perhaps under the circumstances, she'd like to come to us. Instead of going back to that other place.

Avril (*distastefully*) Other place.

Tudor Do you think she'd like that? We've got a spare room.

Miriam (*a moment while she thinks she has summed it all up*) You've been talking to our Maureen, have you?

Tudor Maureen? No. We haven't seen her.

Miriam Today. This morning. You haven't seen her this morning?

Tudor We haven't been out till now.

Avril Now.

Miriam (*after a slight pause*) Well, it's very kind of you both to offer to take her on, but there isn't any need—really.

Tudor Ah but we'd like to.

Avril Like to, yes.

Miriam (*standing*) I know how you feel about sending her back to that "other place". Austin and I have a similar opinion. That's why we've decided to keep her on here.

Tudor (*delighted*) So she's staying with you, then?

Miriam We thought it best.

Tudor Well, I think that's marvellous.

Avril 'Llous.

Miriam I'll remember your offer though, and if you'd like to have her with you from time to time, I'm sure we could arrange something.

Tudor I'm glad you've been able to sort something out. I was saying to Avril——

Avril He was saying, yes.

Tudor I didn't like the thought of Mavis going back to that place all on her own.

Miriam Oh she wasn't short of friends—from what I can gather. Especially the male of the gender.

Tudor Well you know Mavis. She was always one for the boys. When she was younger of course. And she was an attractive little thing too.

Avril (*patting the back of her head*) 'Tractive, yes.

Austin enters

Austin (*to Tudor*) Mavis wants you both in the front-room.

Tudor (*indicating himself and Avril*) Us?

Austin Well she's asking for Torvill and Dean I presume she means you two.

Tudor starts to make towards Avril then he stops, changes his mind and returns to Austin

Tudor (*putting his hand on Austin's shoulder*) I want to thank you for what you're doing for our Mavis. There's not many brothers-in-law that would put themselves out like that. I appreciate that. (*He makes for Avril*) Come on then, Avril. Let's not keep her waiting.

Tudor grabs Avril's elbow and yanks her out of the room

Austin What's he on about? What am I doing for Mavis?
Miriam You're giving her a home.
Austin No I'm not.
Miriam This is my house as well as yours.
Austin You can have it all if she moves in here with us. I'll be moving out.
Miriam (*going to him*) Let me explain it to you.
Austin Nothing you say will make me change my mind.
Miriam (*taking him by the arm*) We've found another letter. It's genuine. Witnessed, dated, the lot. In it, it says that the house and all its contents goes to the sister who will give Mavis a home for the rest of her days. If Mavis comes to live here, that house could be ours. It's got to be worth thirty thousand pounds.
Austin A hundred thousand pounds wouldn't be enough to live with Mavis. What's the point in having all that money if we're crazy.
Miriam We're not crazy—Mavis is.
Austin A month with Mavis and there'll be nothing to choose between any of us.

Miriam breaks away from him

Miriam (*after a pause*) Tudor and Avril have offered to have her.
Austin There you are then—that's you way out of it.
Miriam You must be joking. I'm not lining their pockets with the proceeds of my father's house.
Austin Believe me, Miriam, if they're prepared to take Mavis off our hands for thirty thousand pounds we're having a bargain.
Miriam What I plan to do is this, we'll let Mavis stay here, long enough to sell the house and so on, and then we'll ask Tudor and Avril if they'd like to have her there. They've more or less agreed to that anyway.
Austin (*sighing*) I hope you know what you're doing.
Miriam Trust me.
Austin What about Maureen and Margaret?
Miriam Maureen wouldn't be able to take her on, as much as she'd like to. And it would be out of the question as far as Margaret is concerned.
Austin Where money is involved Margaret is never out of the question.

Margaret enters in a flurry. She is not yet dressed in her funeral clothes. She is quite angry. She has hurried to get there. She has her car keys in her hand

Margaret What's all this about a will?
Miriam Who let you in?

Margaret Josey. I gather you've found an official paper.

Miriam How do you know?

Margaret Maureen told me. I went to see her—I thought it best. I thought I ought to put things right.

Miriam I'm glad you did. You know she wasn't going to come to the funeral?

Margaret Yes, she said. However. (*There is a pause*) Well may I see it? This will?

Miriam Of course. (*She gets it from the cabinet*)

Austin I'll leave you two at it.

Austin exits

Miriam (*going to Margaret*) Did Maureen tell you what's in it?

Margaret She told me that Mavis goes with the house if that's what you mean. (*She takes the will from Miriam and sits in the chair to read it*)

Miriam Well basically, that's all it says. There's not an awful lot of money, but enough I would have thought to cover the funeral expenses.

A pause while Margaret finishes reading

Margaret So what happens now?

Miriam I've discussed the possibility with Maureen of Mavis going there but that's not at all practical, which I fully agree, so that only leaves you and me.

Margaret What are the alternatives?

Miriam Well how I see it is this; she either goes to you, or she *could* come here, or she goes back to where she came from.

Margaret And what would happen to the house if she did the latter?

Miriam If you read it all it tells you that should Mavis return to the home, the house is to be sold and all monies are to be donated to the RSPCA.

Margaret The RSPCA? He hated animals.

Miriam Apparently he must have hated us more.

Margaret I'll kill him.

Miriam Unfortunately mother nature has beaten you to it. Oh, there is one other alternative I've forgotten to mention. Tudor and Avril have offered to have her there.

Margaret (*amazed*) They make me ill. They'll do anything for money. (*Slight pause*) Well there's nothing else for it—she'll have to come to me.

Miriam But she can't do that.

Margaret Why not?

Miriam Well for a start, for all the reasons you couldn't have her for the funeral. No room and Hugh's chest.

Margaret I refuse to let Tudor and whatever her name is get rich on our part. And the thought of all that money going to the cats and dogs repulses me.

Miriam Austin and I have decided to have her here.

Margaret Have you now.

Miriam We thought it best under the circumstances.

Margaret I'm sure you did. And what does Mavis think about it all?

Miriam Oh she's very excited. I've told her she can have her own room.

Margaret With the sale of Father's house you can afford to build her an extension.

Miriam We thought we'd invest it. The monthly income should be quite substantial.

Margaret (*after a pause*) I wonder if I might see Mavis?

Miriam Yes, she's in the front room with the others. Go on in.

Margaret No I meant in private. I don't really want to go in there.

Miriam Can I ask why you want to see her?

Margaret I have a message for her from Father.

Miriam He hasn't come back?

Margaret He whispered it to me.

Miriam Don't tell me—with his dying breath.

Margaret It's a personal message he asked me to convey to her.

Miriam Funny he should ask you.

Margaret (*becoming a little angry*) Yes well there it is. Now I've only got someone to cover me in the shop for half an hour so if you'll kindly get her then I'll go!

They stare at each other for a moment. Miriam decides to control her temper

Miriam (*fuming*) Right.

> *Miriam storms out of the room. Eventually she returns with Mavis, dragging her in by her elbow.*

Miriam puts Mavis near the settee and then stands facing Margaret, waiting for her to deliver the message

Margaret (*to Miriam*) I'll call you, shall I? When I'm leaving?

> *Still in a temper, but beautifully controlled, Miriam leaves the room*

> Hello, Mavis. Do you remember me?

Mavis looks in the opposite direction

> Shall we sit down? (*She goes and sits on the settee*) Aren't you going to join me?

Mavis looks at her. Margaret taps the seat for Mavis to sit next to her. Mavis goes and sits in the armchair opposite

> You're not shy are you? You never used to be. When we were children you were always hanging around me.

Mavis darts her a look

> I mean, I couldn't move without you. We were always together—Father used to call us sugar and spice.

She laughs heartily but it dies when Mavis shows no reaction

> I don't suppose you've missed me, Mavis, but I've certainly missed you. (*She stands*) I used to try not to think about it. It upset me so much to

think of you shut away in that dreadful place—you do realize that, don't you? I vividly remember objecting strongly to Father about it. He convinced me in the end that it was for your own good; but I vowed then that if ever there was a time I could get you out of there I would. So, Mavis, this is your lucky day. (*She goes and kneels by the side of Mavis*) How would you like to come and live with me?

Mavis is still not interested

You'd have your own room. I'd redecorate it and you could have the wallpaper of your own choosing. Would you like that?

No reply

I drive. (*She gets up and moves behind the armchair, dangling her bunch of car keys as she goes*) I have my own car. I could take you places. Places you've never been before. I haven't had a holiday for years. We could go off somewhere—no expense spared (*Kneeling*) Bournemouth perhaps. You'd love it there. What do you say, Mavis. Mmmm?

Mavis is still not showing any interest

(*Getting up and moving in front of Mavis*) You could help me in my shop. I have a baby clothes shop.

Suddenly, Mavis begins to bite

We could serve together. I sell lots of pretty things. White, blue and pink things. Every time I make a sale you can wrap it up in that soft white paper. You'd like that, wouldn't you?

Mavis nods

I'd introduce you to all my customers and teach you to use the phone etc. And when I retire think of all the time we could spend together. We could even go abroad. (*Kneeling again*) Up in an aeroplane. What do you think of that, Mavis? Mmmm? Mavis?

Mavis beams with delight. Then, quite unexpectedly, she blows a wet raspberry in Margaret's face. Black-out

SCENE 2

The same. 1.30 p.m. that day

A dining-chair has been positioned in the space between the armchair and the settee and a box of tissues has been placed on the coffee-table

When the CURTAIN *rises Margaret is sitting in the armchair and Maureen is sitting on the settee with Avril seated next to her and Josey standing behind them. Maureen is upset and she and Avril are holding hands with Avril obviously comforting her. Margaret is expressionless. Josey looks at Margaret and then at Maureen. During the following although no-one says anything, we hear their "thoughts" (pre-recorded voices)*

Josey's thoughts (*meaning Maureen*) She must have got the cleanest eyes in the room. She hasn't stopped crying yet. (*Meaning Margaret*) And she hasn't started. I tell a lie, a couple of tears did fall this morning. Mind you, she was peeling onions at the time.

Margaret's thoughts God, I wonder how long I've got to stay here. (*She looks at Maureen*) She's laying it on a bit thick.

Miriam enters carrying a tray of tea and a plate of corned beef and onion sandwiches. She sets the tray down on the coffee-table and pours tea

Ah, here comes the spread. I don't know who she thinks she is. She's done more with two ounces of cornbeef than Jesus did with five loaves and two fishes. (*After a slight pause*) Or was it two loaves and five fishes?

Miriam hands Margaret a cup of tea. Margaret refuses, putting her hand on her chest

I couldn't possibly drink out of *that* china.

Miriam gives the cup to Avril then returns to the coffee-table to pour more tea

Avril's thoughts (*with cup in one hand and Maureen's hand in the other*) Is she ever going to let go of my hand? I hope she starts pulling herself together.

Maureen's thoughts (*still upset*) I wish I wasn't so upset. I wish I could control myself. (*Snatching her hand away*) And I wish she'd stop squeezing my bloody hand.

Miriam hands Maureen a cup of tea

Josey's thoughts (*moving to sit on the settee*) I lay any odds she won't pour one for me. You watch.

Miriam pours a cup for herself and sits on the dining-chair

See? She never does. I didn't want one anyway.

There is a pause

Miriam's thoughts Well, it didn't go off too badly.

Miriam Help yourself to something to eat.

There is another pause as they all look at each other. Avril is the one to make the first move. She takes up the plate of sandwiches and returns to her seat. As she does we hear Margaret's pre-recorded voice

Margaret's thoughts Yes, grab one quick, Avril. If we all took one each, there'd be nothing left.

Miriam There's plenty there.

Maureen's thoughts Plenty? You can see the pattern on the plate now.

Avril (*offering the plate*) Want one?

Maureen Ay, go on. (*She takes the last three remaining sandwiches*) I'm starving see, and feeding two.

Margaret You haven't taken them all, Maureen?

Maureen I only had three.

Margaret That's over half.

Maureen (*to Miriam*) Pass this over to her. (*She offers a sandwich*)

Margaret No, I don't want it now.

Maureen Are you being funny?

Margaret Not at all.

Maureen My hands are clean. I washed them when I got up this morning. (*To Miriam*) Pass this to her.

Margaret I don't want it I said.

Maureen (*to Miriam*) She is being funny, I don't care what she says. (*To Margaret*) Are you going to have it now? This is your last chance.

Margaret No, thank you.

Maureen Oh, please your bloody self then. (*She rams it in her mouth*)

Miriam I hope you two are not going to start today.

Maureen (*with her mouth full*) Well, it's her, it is. She said about me having them all and then she didn't want one.

They all look at each other because no-one has understood a word. Maureen glares at Miriam, having swallowed the sandwich

And where's the pork pie I fetched?

Miriam I'm keeping it for the others.

Margaret Bring it out. We'll have it now.

Miriam But there'll be nothing left.

Maureen I'm not going to eat it all.

Miriam Wait for the rest to come.

Maureen (*determined*) It's my pie and we'll have it now.

Miriam (*reluctantly*) Well, there'll be nothing left for the men.

Miriam goes to the kitchen

Maureen (*calling after her*) They're only six. Open that box of Kraft cheeses Margaret fetched. (*To Avril*) She's probably saving them for Austin's supper.

Margaret And she had the gall to call me thrifty.

Avril (*after a slight pause*) I had a meat hamper in the house. If I'd known, I could have brought that over.

Margaret Never mind. Keep it for the next funeral.

Avril Next one, yes. Makes you wonder who the next one will be, doesn't it?

Maureen (*shuddering*) Ooh, it's not nice to think about.

Margaret I wouldn't be at all surprised if it's Hugh. He's not as young as he used to be and his chest is definitely getting worse.

Maureen That's the only thing about marrying an older man. Chances are he'll go before you.

Margaret I'm not too concerned. I've taken ample precautions—he's heavily insured.

Avril and Maureen share a look

Miriam enters with a plate of pork pie and hands it to Maureen

Maureen takes a piece and offers it to the rest of the room

Maureen Anyone?

No-one answers

(*Handing the plate to Avril and indicating the coffee-table*) Shove that on there for me, luv.

Avril does so

Miriam That's a pretty dress, Avril.
Avril (*doing a twirl*) Like it? I run it up yesterday.
Maureen (*showing off*) I got a new cardigan.
Margaret Yes, I was just admiring it.
Maureen I'm sending it back tomorrow.
Margaret Yes, it's flawed, isn't it? I can see it from here.
Maureen (*insulted*) No, it's not flawed.
Margaret Then, why are you sending it back?
Maureen 'Cos I had it from the catalogue.
Margaret (*after a slight pause*) I have people like you in the shop. Want to take the christening-gown home, to see if it fits the baby. I fell for it once or twice. Bring the baby here is what I tell them now. I'd drop that catalogue if I were you, Maureen. It only encourages people to buy things they can't afford.
Maureen What else is a catalogue for? And I haven't got the money to pay cash. And don't you go knocking the catalogue. Mammy had one for years—she had to—to keep you in knickers.
Margaret (*disgusted*) Really!
Maureen It's true, isn't it, Miriam?

Miriam covers a smile and nods

(*To Avril and Josey*) We always used to have something in turns. If we'd been good, she'd let us pick something for ourselves. (*To Miriam*) What did I always choose now?
Miriam A torch.
Maureen That's right. I used to have it for the dark nights, 'cos if Mammy wanted anything down the shop it was always *me* who had to go. (*To Miriam*) You always used to ask for brassières. You never had one, but you always asked.
Margaret What did I used to ask for?
Maureen I told you, knickers. You were obsessed with them. (*She laughs*) We went hunting in her bedroom once. I can't remember what we were looking for now, probably nothing, but we used to like to creep in to see what she had.

Margaret looks disgusted

And there was this chest—(*to Miriam*) remember?—with three or four drawers in it. When we opened them, they were all full of knickers. The four of them. Drawers full of drawers.
Miriam (*laughing*) I bet she's still the same.
Maureen No, she's not. She doesn't wear them now.

Margaret glares at her

I was only joking. If you've got a couple of pairs to spare though, Margaret, I'll take them off you. I'm a bit low on smalls.

Margaret The ones I wear wouldn't be suitable for you.

Maureen Why not? Got reinforced gussets, have they?

They all laugh, except Margaret who looks away

(*To Miriam*) I love teasing her. (*After a pause*) We'll be all right, Miriam. Think of all the underwear we'll have if anything happens to her.

Margaret No-one is having anything after me.

Miriam Taking it all with you, are you?

Margaret I'm working on it.

Maureen (*after a slight pause*) And if your Hugh should go first, like you said—that suit he's wearing today would fit our Des lovely.

Margaret Yes, Hugh is marvellous on his clothes. He looks after them so well. That suit you're talking about is the same one he got married in.

Miriam I thought it was. And the colour was so right for that occasion. (*She mouths the word "black" to the others*)

Margaret Twice it's been cleaned since he bought it. That's sixteen years.

Miriam Well, they hardly get dirty when they're only used for weddings and funerals.

Margaret It's been worth every penny he paid for it.

Miriam Made to measure, then? Or was it Oxfam?

Maureen I can see our Des in that suit.

Margaret Well, he's not having it. Should anything happen to Hugh, he'll be buried in it.

Miriam Good idea. Especially with the price of shrouds today.

Margaret How much does a good funeral cost these days?

Miriam (*thinking*) Oh—about five, six hundred pounds.

Margaret As much as that? It'll get to the stage soon where you won't be able to afford to die. And I don't know what you're going to do then, Maureen, because you can't get that from the catalogue.

Maureen The State can bury me—or they can dump me at sea.

Margaret With all that nuclear waste?

Maureen No, I wasn't thinking that far out. Just off Barry Docks will do.

Margaret What if you come back in with the tide?

Maureen Then they can bury me in the sand. Let the crabs have me. I'm not bothered.

Margaret I can see you're going to be another burden to the taxpayer.

Maureen Ay, why not? (*A thought strikes her*) You're a taxpayer, aren't you?

Margaret Of course.

Maureen Well, that's all right then. (*To Miriam*) I'm determined to have something out of her.

Avril (*after a pause*) Me and Tudor——

They all look at her

—are going to leave our bodies to science.

Maureen Do you think they'll want them?

Avril Tudor has got marvellous *feet*. Our doctor says they should be preserved. Be made a specimen of.

Miriam They'll have to preserve the wellies as well then.

Maureen Ooh, I can see those feet in a glass case. (*She shudders*)

Margaret And what are they going to try to preserve of you?

Avril Nothing. I did suggest they try to preserve all of me, but they said it wasn't practical.

Maureen Why not? I would have thought it would be the easiest thing in the world to stick you on a shelf somewhere in a bucketful of brine.

Avril (*confidentially*) No, listen, I'm going to be dissected by thirty-five students.

Miriam Doesn't the thought of all those young men looking at you put you off?

Avril Not at all.

They all scream with laughter, except Margaret

Margaret Aren't we forgetting what day it is?

Maureen (*momentarily confused*) It's Thursday.

Margaret It's the day of our father's funeral. Let's talk about something else.

There is a pause in which Maureen offers around cigarettes. She throws one to Josey while Miriam gets the lighter from the small table. She lights Maureen's cigarette, then her own

Maureen I thought he looked so peaceful when I saw him earlier.

Margaret You should have seen him after I took Mavis in there.

Avril What happened. No-one has said.

Margaret His expression changed. Mavis threw a fit.

Miriam She had a turn, that's all. Which was quite understandable. She didn't know she was coming home to a funeral.

Maureen You should have told her on Saturday, as soon as she got here. Poor bugger thought she was going on holiday. I ought to go up and have a look at her, I haven't seen her since she's home. I think I'll nip up now.

Miriam No, leave her where she is Maureen. She's all right, I went up just before the service. She's heavily sedated. I told the doctor to inject her with enough Valium to knock her out till the weekend.

Maureen She's sleeping then?

Miriam Like a baby.

There is a knock at the front door

Answer that, Josey.

Josey Nuh—(*she takes a tissue from the box*)—I'm in mourning!

Miriam exits

Maureen Talking about babies, this bugger's kicking hell out of me.

Margaret Perhaps it wants to come out.

Maureen No, I'm not due for another fortnight.

Margaret What are you hoping for?

Maureen I don't mind. It'll probably look like Desmond whatever it is.
Avril She'd like another boy really, wouldn't you?
Margaret If you have a little girl and you name her Margaret—I could be persuaded to be a godparent.
Maureen You bugger off. One Margaret is enough in our house.
Margaret Who do you have by the name of Margaret living with you?
Maureen Our cat. (*She laughs*)

Mansel storms into the room followed by Miriam. He is very upset. He sits down and covers his face with his hands

Maureen What the hell's the matter with him?
Margaret Is he on his own, Miriam?
Miriam No, the others are coming.

Conversation is heard from Austin and Tudor as they enter the room. Tudor is wheeling Mansel's shopping trolley. He still wears his wellingtons

Austin Where's Margaret?
Miriam What's the matter with Mansel?
Austin He'll be all right in a minute.
Tudor Here you are. I've brought it in for you, look. (*He puts the trolley next to Mansel*)

Mansel doesn't react, he remains seated with his hands covering his face

Desmond comes in. He is smoking and carrying a crateful of cider

Desmond Gangway!
Miriam (*to Desmond*) Where do you think you're going with that?
Desmond It's only a couple of flagons, that's all.
Miriam Well, what's it for?
Desmond For us to have a drink. You know—wet the corpse's head.

There is a deadly silence

Maureen (*scornfully*) Desmond!
Desmond Well, he would have wanted that. I'll put it up here for now. (*He puts it on floor* UC)
Margaret Did you want me, Austin?
Austin Er—yes. Now don't get frightened. There's been a bit of an accident.
Margaret Is it Hugh?
Austin I'm afraid so.
Maureen Hey, I bagged that suit first.
Margaret (*getting hysterical*) What's happened to him? Is he dead? What hospital have they taken him to?
Austin Well, they haven't taken him to hospital.
Margaret You've never left him in the cemetery?
Austin We nearly did. No—he's in the passage. He's afraid to come in.
Margaret What has he done?
Austin Now, he couldn't help it. An accident it was, after all.

There is a bubble of conversation which gets louder until stopped by Margaret shouting

Margaret Hugh!!

All look at her

If I were you, I'd get in here a bit quick and start confessing.

They all turn, except Mansel, to the door as

Hugh comes into the room. He is covered in mud, even his face. He doesn't say anything. It's all he can do to get his breath. He is in shock

Look at you. What the hell have you done to your suit? It's ruined, ruined. Go into the kitchen. This is all I need. Trust you to do something like this. Don't try and tell me—I don't want to know. You can take all those clothes off for a start.

Margaret and Hugh exit to the kitchen

Miriam Well, what's been going on then?

Tudor I was there. I saw it. One minute he was standing next to me and the next he was laying alongside his father-in-law. I had an idea they were close, but I didn't know they were that thick. Someone said he slipped. Well, lucky he was that I happened to have my wellingtons on, 'cos no-one would venture down to get him back up. Afraid to get their shoes dirty of course. And I nearly put my shoes on, didn't I, Avril, only I thought better of it.

Avril Of it, yes.

Tudor And it was a new grave, see. Six feet. It's a long way to fall.

Miriam Do you think he's broken anything?

Tudor Well, look now. (*He searches through his pockets*) I found these in the mud. (*He reveals a top set of dentures*) Look, the plate has snapped clean in half.

Miriam But Hugh doesn't wear dentures.

Tudor (*after a pause*) Well, whose are these then?

Mansel (*taking his hands from his face*) They're mine. And I don't want them back now, not since they've been floating in the grave. (*He puts his hands back over his face*)

Miriam So that's what's wrong with him?

Mansel (*taking his hands from his face again*) No, it's not. I don't care about my teeth, but they're not doing what they like with my dog. (*He puts his hands back over his face again*)

Tudor (*explaining*) Trolley.

Miriam What's he on about?

Margaret enters from the kitchen

Margaret All right, come on. Let's have it out.

Miriam What?

Margaret Hugh has just told me what happened. And according to him he didn't slip at all—he was pushed.

Miriam and Maureen exchange a look

Now, you may as well know it, I have no intention of leaving this room until I find out who did it. So come on, own up. Who's the culprit?

They all look at Desmond. He is laughing to himself. Suddenly, he is aware of the attention

Desmond It wasn't me. I didn't do it.

Tudor coughs to get everyone's attention. He points with his thumb to Mansel

Tudor (*mouthing the words*) It was him. I saw him. (*He mimes the push*)
Margaret Was it you, Mansel?
Miriam Oh, you won't get anything out of him now. Not when he's like that.
Desmond I hate to break up anything—but has anybody got a bottle opener?
Austin I'll get one, Des.

Austin exits to the kitchen

Margaret Hugh is very upset. The whole business has taken ten years off his life.
Maureen According to you, he didn't have ten years left in him.
Mansel (*taking his hands from his face*) It was me. I did it. It was his own fault. He took my dog off me. (*He puts his hands to his face again*)
Tudor Trolley. He wanted to take it in the car but there was no room. He didn't like it then because Hugh made him put it in the boot. He had a tap 'cos he couldn't get in there with it.
Margaret Well, I think it's disgusting. (*To Miriam*) From what I can see, your family's loopy on both sides.

Austin enters from the kitchen

Austin Here you are, Des. (*He throws the bottle opener to Desmond*) By the way, I wouldn't advise any of you ladies to go in the kitchen. Hugh is in there with nothing on. (*To Margaret*) He told me to ask you to hurry up, his feet are getting cold. (*To Miriam*) Better get him my bathrobe, Miriam.

Margaret and Miriam exit to the kitchen

Right, then. Glasses. They should be in here. (*He goes to the cabinet*)
Desmond Cider it is. Does that suit everyone? Tudor? Mansel?
Maureen You can pour me a glass, I'm parched.
Desmond What are the ladies going to have?
Maureen I'll have a cider, I said.
Desmond I wasn't asking you, I was asking the ladies.
Tudor Avril will have a sherry.
Avril Sherry, yes.
Desmond Right, so it's cider for the men and sherry for the ladies.
Tudor Do you want a drop of cider, Manse?

Mansel doesn't answer—his face is still covered

Come on, don't be like that. It's all over now and you had er . . . (*pointing to the trolley*) Rover back, didn't you?

Mansel (*covering his face*) But we go everywhere together. He pines awful if he can't come with me.

Tudor Put your hands down, I can't hear you.

Mansel does so

Now, what did you say?

Mansel I'll have a cider.

Maureen (*after a slight pause*) Apart from Hugh, how did everything go off at the cemetery?

Desmond Great. Lovely service. And the old man went down like a trooper.

Tudor Does he give his paw?

Mansel I'm training him now. He can beg though, watch. (*He takes the trolley by the handle and tilts it forward about forty-five degrees*) Beg, then. Go on, beg for Dad. One, two, three. (*On "three" he flicks the trolley with his hand and it reverts to its upright position*) See?

Austin and Desmond laugh. Tudor is amazed. He looks around the room for agreed astonishment in the others but everyone, except Avril, is only astonished that Tudor has been taken in by it

Avril That was marvellous. How did you get him to do that?

Mansel Took hours of training.

Desmond You want to keep your eye on it. It'll be cocking its leg up against the furniture next.

Mansel No he won't. Anyway, he's house trained.

Miriam enters from the kitchen

Maureen (*to Miriam*) How's everything out there?

Miriam Oh, I feel sorry for him. Do you know, she's more concerned about the suit than she is about Hugh.

Desmond Yes, I'd let my wife speak to me like that. She'd have the back of my hand.

Maureen And if my husband clouted me, he'd have a bugger back too.

Desmond blows her a kiss. Maureen makes a face as if it makes her vomit

Austin Well, I'm the boss in our house, aren't I, Miriam?

Miriam (*humouring him*) You. Yes, that's right.

Tudor I don't know whether I ought to say anything. Avril thinks *she's* the boss but likes to believe she thinks she knows *I* am. And I know I'm not but let her think she believes I could be. And of course I am. Or so I'd have her think she believes. On the other hand, when people outside ask, we both know we think each other is. But we're always wrong, aren't we, Avril?

Avril Always wrong, yes, that's right.

Desmond Here you are then. (*To Austin*) Help me pass these around.

They give out the drinks

Miriam Let's drink a toast. I'll call the others. (*Calling to the kitchen*) Margaret, we're going to drink a toast to Father, are you going to join us?
Margaret (*off*) I can't at the moment, I'm busy. Toast him without me.
Miriam What about Hugh?
Margaret (*off*) I'll send him in when he's ready.
Austin (*raising his glass*) To the old man.

They all raise their glasses. Each of them mumbles "Dad", "Father" or whatever they called the old man

Hugh comes in from the kitchen. He wears Austin's bathrobe and his shoes and socks

Hugh Have I missed anything?
Desmond Here's your drink. (*He hands it to him*)

Hugh is about to drink when Margaret calls from the kitchen

Margaret (*off*) I hope you're saying no to that drink they're handing round, Hugh.
Desmond (*loud enough for Margaret to hear*) Sure you won't join us, Hugh?

Desmond makes a face at him. Hugh catches on and answers equally as loud

Hugh No, I never touch the stuff.

They laugh quietly. From this point on the people divide into little groups. There is a general chit-chat before we hear the conversation between Hugh and Miriam R

Miriam Are you feeling better now, Hugh?
Hugh Just about I think.
Miriam Do you want to sit down?
Hugh No, it's easier to breathe standing up. (*He uses his pump*)
Miriam Your suit will be all right once she's finished sponging it down.
Hugh Sponging it down? She's soaking it in the bloody sink.

Miriam moves away

Avril No-one has touched our Tudor's almond cake. (*To Maureen*) Try a piece.
Maureen No thanks, I don't like almonds.
Avril Well, that's all right, 'cos there's none in there anyway.
Maureen You have a piece.
Avril No, I won't bother. (*Confidentially*) Between you and me, I don't like it. But I can't go telling him that now can I?
Tudor (*to Mansel*) It's easy, a chimpanzee can do it. All you need is two cups of flour, a cup of sugar, eight ounces of marge, three ounces of sliced almonds and a drop of milk. Carnation will do if you haven't got any fresh.
Desmond I mean I would have come in after you in a minute—but I couldn't pull myself together. You have to admit, it was so bloody funny.

Hugh Funny? I didn't think it was funny.

Austin Even the vicar laughed.

Desmond Now he surprised me. I wouldn't have thought he'd see the funny side of it.

Austin Funny side of it? If you hadn't slapped his face, he would have been hysterical.

Desmond I'm still not sure I should have done that.

Austin What else could you do?

Desmond He's full of surprises mind, for a vicar. The last thing I expected was for him to slap me back. (*He feels the side of his face*)

They all laugh

Margaret enters and goes to Hugh

Margaret Whose drink is that?

Hugh is speechless

Desmond Mine. He's holding it for me.

Margaret And whose is that? (*She points to the drink he is already holding*)

Desmond Er—the vicar's.

Margaret The vicar isn't here.

Desmond Yes he is. (*To Austin*) Isn't he?

Austin Er—yes. He's upstairs.

Margaret (*suspiciously*) What's he doing up there?

Austin I don't know. Probably gone up to look in on Mavis.

Margaret is suspicious. She doesn't really believe any of it

Avril leaves the room

Miriam joins Maureen

Mansel I always thought you had to put eggs in a cake?

Tudor No, you haven't got to, not in this one. You haven't even got to put almonds in if you don't want to. Try a piece. (*He hands him the plate*)

Miriam It's all over then, bar the shouting.

Maureen Ay. And if I know our lot, there'll be plenty more of that.

Miriam Oh, I don't know if I've got any fight left in me.

Mavis enters. She is amazed at the sight of so many people. She beams at the prospect of introducing herself to them. She wastes no time and begins immediately with Hugh, Desmond, etc.

And from what I can see, it's pointless anyway. When it comes down to the nitty-gritty, she's better at it than I am. That's why she always wins. Between you and me, I had it all planned. She was going to have Mavis and our father—and what happens? You toss a bloody coin and I end up with both of them.

Maureen Well, it was the only thing I could think of. If I'd left it to you two, the poor bugger would have gone from the garage.

Miriam I'll have her one day though. I don't know how but one of these days I'll have her.

Maureen What do you mean? Like throw a brick through her shop window?

Miriam No, nothing like that.

Maureen Well, say what you mean.

Miriam (*brushing it off*) Oh, I don't know.

Maureen Hey, I've got plenty of bricks in my house if you want one.

Miriam No. Much as I'd like to, I'd never have the guts to do something like that.

Maureen Well, give our Rupert fifty pence. He'll do it for you.

Mavis is now with Margaret

Margaret Hello, Mavis. How are you feeling? Are you better?

Mavis Have you been bad then?

Margaret Not me—you.

Mavis You I mean.

Margaret (*after a pause*) You're feeling all right now? Good, I am glad.

Mavis Are you sure? You're not looking very good. Do you want to have my key? You can go and have a lie down in my room if you want to. (*She starts to look for the key in her bag*)

Margaret (*stopping her*) No, no. It's all right. Don't bother.

Mavis Just as well. 'Cos I haven't got a key anyway. You take care of yourself. Doing too much you are I expect.

Mavis sees Miriam and Maureen and goes to them

Mavis Hello.

Miriam (*surprised*) What are you doing up? You're supposed to be knocked out.

Maureen Knocked out?

Mavis (*to Miriam*) You didn't tell me it was market day—and all these people. (*To Maureen, indicating Miriam*) What do you think of her as a warden?

Maureen (*puzzled*) Warden?

Mavis I don't like her myself. (*She sits on the arm of the settee*) She pinched all my pills. Don't you let her have yours.

Maureen I haven't got any pills.

Mavis Taken them all have you? Well, see me after and I'll give you some of mine. Excuse me. (*She goes to talk to Mansel and Tudor*)

Maureen (*to Miriam*) What the hell is she on about?

Miriam Her birth pills. It's a long story.

Maureen Who is God's name is she anyway?

Miriam What do you mean?

Maureen Who's she with? Is Mansel courting?

Miriam Courting Mavis?

Maureen No, not Mavis. (*Pointing to Mavis*) Her.

Miriam (*puzzled*) Well, that is Mavis.

Maureen (*after a pause*) What are you on about?

Miriam Mavis. Our sister.

Maureen looks at Mavis then back to Miriam

Maureen That's not Mavis. Our Mavis is nothing like that.

There is a shocked pause. For a moment, Miriam asks herself what has happened. Then she works it out and screams with infuriation

Miriam Tudor!!

Everyone turns to look at Tudor. He has just bitten off a mouthful of cake. He turns to Miriam. Black-out

CURTAIN

SCENE 3

The same. Later that afternoon

When the CURTAIN *rises Miriam is on the telephone. Margaret is tapping her fingers impatiently. Maureen is taking off her shoes—her feet are killing her. Mavis is sitting in the armchair. She is wearing her coat and gloves and her suitcase is beside her. She is ready to leave*

Miriam Yes I know that. You keep telling me. But the fact is, no-one has arrived yet. . . . Well, if she left three-quarters of an hour ago, surely she should be here by now. . . . Well, I'm giving her another ten minutes. If she's not here by then I'm calling the police. (*She hangs up*) They still insist she's on her way.

Maureen Hell, I hope nothing has happened to her.

Margaret I still fail to see how all this could have happened in the first place.

Miriam Oh, I don't know. It's an easy mistake to make. For Tudor.

Maureen Now you can't put all the blame on him. She fooled you two as well.

Margaret You're right. (*To Miriam*) You should have realized. It would have saved us a lot of bother if you had.

Miriam You're just as guilty for not recognizing her as I am.

Maureen What bother?

Margaret Well—I needn't have taken the trouble to—er—to . . .

Miriam Pass on Father's message?

Margaret Yes.

Miriam You may as well tell us what it is now. It can't be that personal if you've told her. (*She indicates Mavis*)

Mavis I wish you wouldn't keep talking about me as if I was here.

Margaret I'm afraid my lips are sealed.

Miriam I'll ask Mavis to tell us if you won't.

Margaret Mavis won't say anything if I ask her not to.

Miriam (*kneeling beside Mavis's chair*) Tell me what Margaret told you earlier.

Margaret Say nothing, Mavis.

Mavis Nothing.

Maureen I don't know why you're bothering. Whatever Margaret has told her won't make any sense if she repeats it.

Miriam (*getting up*) True. Oh, I don't think I'll be so glad as when I see our own Mavis. (*She sits on arm of the settee*)

Maureen Hey, let me tell you something. Our Mavis is worse than that.

Margaret Can they come any worse?

Maureen With a bit of luck, you won't have to wait long to find out.

Margaret (*turning to Miriam*) Bearing that little piece of information in mind—do you still want to stick to our agreement?

Miriam (*moving round the back of the settee*) Of course I do. I'm far more likely to cope with Mavis than you are.

Margaret How can you say that after the last time?

Miriam I was younger then.

Margaret I would have thought that that would have been an asset.

Miriam Well, in that case we two are at an advantage. You're the oldest.

Margaret is at a loss for words

So it's still four months each with Mavis and the sale of the house split three ways.

Maureen I don't want to put a damper on things but we still haven't decided who's having Mavis first.

Margaret It's difficult for me to have her straight away. It's the end of my financial year. I'm up to my neck in stocktaking.

Miriam Well Maureen's not having her, not with the baby coming. And that only leaves you and me, so I don't know what to suggest. But I know one thing for sure, I ain't tossing no bloody coin.

Mavis (*after a slight pause*) They quarrel like that over me in the other place.

They all look at her

Miriam Who do?

Mavis The men.

Miriam (*to Maureen*) I can't imagine any man quarrelling over her.

Maureen Oh, I can. They'll quarrel over anything there—ash trays, door knobs—you name it. I went there once and there were these two men quarrelling over the moon. One said it was his and the other one wanted to take it down out of the sky and eat it. You should have been there. There was ructions.

Miriam (*facing Margaret*) Well, Margaret, I suggest you either postpone your stocktaking or get Mavis to give you a hand.

Mavis Yes. I'll take your stock for you.

Miriam I didn't mean you, I meant Mavis.

Mavis Who am I then?

Maureen You're the other Mavis.

Mavis (*after a slight pause*) The other Mavis is where I used to live.

Maureen That's right.

Mavis How is it I'm here then?

Miriam (*moving towards Mavis*) You're a mistake.

Margaret You can say that again.

Mavis If I'm the other Mavis, I shouldn't be here.

Miriam You're going home soon. The warden is coming to fetch you.

Mavis (*to Miriam*) So you're not going to be my warden any more then, are you?

Miriam No.

Mavis Good. (*To the others*) 'Cos she's 'orrible anyway.

Hugh appears in the room. He has come from the front room where all the men are having a drink. He stands UC. He is drunk

Margaret I hope those men are behaving themselves in there.

Miriam notices Hugh

I've warned Hugh not to have anything stronger than a shandy.

Hugh hiccups. Margaret thinks it's Maureen. Miriam begins slowly backing up towards Hugh

Hold your breath, Maureen, and count to ten.

Maureen What for?

Margaret It will stop your hiccups.

Maureen I haven't got hiccups.

Miriam guides Hugh out of the room

Margaret It must have been Miriam then.

Miriam comes back into the room

Miriam Yes, yes that's right, it was me.

Suddenly, Mavis hiccups

Maureen You've got her at it now.

Miriam Look, I hate to be a bore, but we still haven't sorted out Mavis. Our Mavis.

Margaret We'll draw straws.

Miriam We'll do no such thing. I'm having my own way for once. (*Firmly*) Margaret, she's going to you. You are having her.

Margaret (*after a slight pause*) Oh, all right again.

Miriam and Maureen look at each other in amazement. Mavis hiccups

Maybe it's best to have her first. At least I won't have her for Christmas.

Miriam And just you remember, no funny business.

Margaret I'm sure I don't know what you mean.

Miriam I mean taking the cheque with one hand and shaking hands with the other because you're emigrating.

Margaret As if I would. Mind you, it is a thought.

Miriam No-one leaves the country until something happens to Mavis.

Margaret That doesn't mean we can't go on holidays, surely.

Miriam No, you can go on holidays, but you take her with you.

Margaret (*rising and moving towards Mavis*) Hugh and I have decided to go to Istanbul. Can you imagine Mavis in Istanbul.

Miriam Of course I can. Just as sure as I can imagine her here with me for Christmas.

Tudor enters, waving a white hanky

Tudor It's me it is. All right to come in? (*He laughs and puts his hanky away*) She hasn't come yet then? Mavis?

Mavis Here I am.

Tudor Hello, love. (*To Miriam*) Not her. I meant the one I should have fetched when I fetched her.

Miriam No, but she's due anytime, so I'd be very grateful if you'd either go back in the other room out of harm's way, or go home.

Tudor Oh, don't be like that. A mistake it was after all. Trying to help out I was.

Maureen How's Mansel, Tudor?

Tudor All right.

Maureen And the trolley.

Tudor Ay. He can make the bloody thing bark now.

Margaret I hope Hugh is behaving himself in there.

Tudor (*going to Margaret*) Hugh. He's a boy, isn't he? Dark horse there.

Margaret Dark horse?

Miriam (*taking Tudor by the arm*) I think you'd better go back in now, Tudor, before you cause any more trouble.

Tudor Am I forgiven then?

Miriam (*struggling to push him out*) Yes, yes all right.

Tudor You'll give me a shout when she comes won't you? Mavis. I want to have a reading, see. (*He mimes the word "spiritualist"*)

Tudor goes out

Maureen What's he on about?

Miriam He's convinced Mavis is a spiritualist.

Margaret Why would he think that?

Miriam Something I said to him a few days ago. He's got his wires crossed.

Margaret He's had his wires crossed for years. I sometimes wonder if this family put the right one away.

Maureen Hey, just to keep the record straight. This family didn't put Mavis away—you did.

Mavis looks at Margaret

Margaret I had very little to do with it. In fact, as I remember, it was you, Miriam, who had the most to say.

Miriam You signed the papers.

Margaret I witnessed Father's signature, that's all. Anyway, does it really matter who signed the damn thing. We all agreed it was for the best.

Maureen I didn't. I would have had her come to me, but I was big in the way with Anthony.

Margaret Well, it's as much your fault as it was mine in that case. If you had exercised a little more control over Desmond with regard to his "nocturnal habits", things might have turned out quite differently.

Maureen Hey, don't you call Desmond "nocturnal". He might walk a bit funny, but that's because he's got a dropped arch.

Margaret and Miriam laugh at Maureen's ignorance of the word nocturnal

What are you two laughing at?

Miriam Nocturnal means in the night. (*She laughs helplessly*)

Maureen quickly thinks over what Margaret has said—putting the right meaning to the word

Maureen What me and Desmond do in the night is no different from any other normal married couple.

Margaret I certainly don't indulge in that sort of thing.

Maureen Any other *normal* married couple, I said. And for your information, I fell for our Anthony one Sunday afternoon—three-quarters of an hour after dinner. He didn't even give me time to do the bloody dishes.

Mavis (*to Margaret*) Did you put me away?

Margaret No, I didn't, but thank God somebody did.

Mavis It was you, wasn't it?

Margaret Of course not, I'm not even your sister.

Mavis (*to Maureen and Miriam*) I'm not going to go and live with her. (*To Margaret*) You can stick your blue and pink things and your soft white paper. (*To the others*) And she can answer her own phone too.

Margaret looks embarrassed

Miriam (*to Margaret*) What have you been promising her?

Margaret I don't know what she's talking about. She's confused.

Miriam It wouldn't have anything to do with the personal message from Father, would it?

Mavis I don't want to go up in an aeroplane anyway. And I've been to Bourneville before.

Margaret (*correcting her*) Bournemouth.

Miriam (*to Maureen*) You can see what she's done, can't you? Promised her the earth just to get her to go and live with her.

Maureen I thought we were having her for four months each.

Miriam We are now. But she asked to see Mavis on her own this morning. Tried to pull the wool over my eyes by telling me she had a personal message from Father.

There is a knock at the door

Personal, my foot. She just wanted the opportunity to get Mavis to see things her way. Didn't do any good though, did it?

Margaret No, because you got in first with your two pence worth.

Maureen Well, it's all water under the bridge now anyway, if we're splitting everything three ways.

Margaret (*to Maureen*) I dread to think what you're going to do with your share.

Maureen Well, one thing's for sure. I won't spend a bloody penny of it in your shop.

Austin enters

Austin Er—she's here. (*He steps aside*)

A woman, the Warden, enters leading Mavis 2 (the real Mavis) with one hand and carrying her suitcase in the other

Warden (*to Margaret*) Mrs Miriam Oliver?
Miriam Yes.
Warden (*turning to Miriam*) Sybil Braithwaite. Administrator, Fair Lawns.
Miriam How do you do.

They shake hands

Warden I'll be brief. I imagine you are upset with the recent bereavement. Obviously an explanation is required. May I speak freely?
Margaret Yes, we're all family. Unfortunately.
Warden Apparently an error in our administration department, which was made some time ago when Mavis was first admitted, has caused this unfortunate situation. On the day that Mavis arrived at Fair Lawns, another Mavis was also admitted the same morning. (*Gesturing to Mavis 1*) Mavis Brindley. (*Gesturing to Mavis 2*) Mavis Bradley. So you see, I'm afraid this whole business is the result of an inexperienced clerk and a rather antiquated Underwood typewriter.

Pause. The Warden gives an embarrassed laugh

If it's any consolation, a similar situation occurred some yars ago with a Ron Merry and a Don Berry.

Pause. Another embarrassed laugh

Well, as I say, I am most dreadfully sorry for any inconvenience caused. This is your correct sister.
Miriam (*to Mavis 2*) Hello, Mavis.

There is no reaction

Warden I hope our other friend hasn't been too much of a problem.
Mavis 1 I'm no problem.
Warden I see she's all packed and ready, so I won't keep you. Come along, Mavis.

Mavis 1 stands

When can we expect your sister to be returned?
Margaret We've decided to keep her here.
Warden She's going to live with you?
Miriam With all of us.
Maureen She's going to be shared out.
Warden Well, I am pleased. Did you hear that, Mavis? You're going to have a new home.

Mavis 2 looks vacant

Live with all your sisters.

Mavis 1 Hey, Mave, I wouldn't live with them. They all seem a bit funny to me. Keep an eye on your handbag and don't let her (*she indicates Miriam*) take your tablets off you.

Miriam Tablets?

Warden They're in her suitcase.

Miriam She's not on the pill as well, is she?

Warden No, they're anti-depressants. Give as directed on the bottle. (*After a slight pause*) I had no idea you had decided to take Mavis on. There are release papers to be signed and so on, but I won't trouble you with all that now. I'll come and see you in a few days and bring them with me.

Mavis 1 (*to the Warden*) I haven't got to come back here, have I?

Warden No.

Mavis 1 That's all right then.

Warden Haven't you enjoyed your stay?

Mavis 1 No, I haven't. They're all bloody cuckoo here.

Warden Now Mavis, you know you're not allowed to say words like that.

Mavis 1 All right. Bloody crazy then.

Warden Bring your case.

Mavis 1 fetches it

I'll ring you to arrange a visit one day next week.

Mavis 1 Ta-ra then.

No-one answers

Ta-ra. (*To the Warden*) See, cuckoo. (*To Mavis 2*) Don't let them get you down, Mave, that's the main thing. And if that one over there (*she indicates Margaret*) offers you a job serving in her shop, tell her you won't do it for under a fiver. (*To the Warden*) Come on, let's go. I've had a bloody gutsful of it here.

Mavis 1 takes the Warden by the arm and marches her out, ad libbing as they go. Austin follows them out

Miriam (*sitting on the settee*) I feel quite numb.

Margaret (*to Mavis 2, all smiles*) Hello Mavis.

No reaction

Maureen (*to Mavis 2*) Come and sit by here, luv.

Mavis 2 doesn't move

Margaret You don't seem to be getting through, Maureen.

Miriam She feels a bit strange I expect. (*To Mavis*) Would you like to sit here, Mavis? (*She taps the seat next to her*)

Margaret Perhaps she's shy.

Maureen She's not usually this quiet. (*She goes to Mavis*) Come on, luv. Come and sit by Mo. (*She leads Mavis to the settee and sits her down*) There you are. (*To Miriam and Margaret*) It'll probably take her a day or two to come round.

Margaret Leave her as she is. I think I could manage her quite well like that.

Hugh enters. He is very drunk

Hugh Where is she?

Margaret looks at him, horrified

Margaret What on earth have you ... I thought I said ... I think you'd better go and ...
Hugh (*shouting*) Shut up.
Margaret I beg your pardon.
Hugh I said, shut up.
Margaret You're drunk.
Hugh I've had a drink, yes, and now I'm ready to go home.
Margaret You'll go home when I tell you.
Hugh Gone are the days, Margaret, when you tell me what to do. I'm ready to go now, so fetch your coat and get the car.

Margaret starts to interrupt

And I don't want no arguments. You'll do as I say now.
Margaret But I can't go, not at the moment. Mavis has only just arrived.
Hugh You can come over and see her again. Home.
Margaret You don't understand. Mavis isn't ready to come with me yet.
Hugh Come with you where?
Margaret She's staying with us for a few months. It's an arrangement we girls have made together.
Hugh Then you can re-arrange it. There's nobody going to live in our house except (*pointing to Margaret*) me and (*pointing to himself*) you.
Margaret But she has to come.
Hugh (*shouting*) I'm not telling you again.
Margaret (*in desperation*) If she doesn't, I'll lose my share of Father's house.
Hugh Then lose it. Lose it. You've got more money now than you need anyway.

Miriam and Maureen share a look

Things are going to change from now on, Margaret. From now on there's going to be a new me. A new Hugh. I'm going to the door. Follow me. If you're not out in two minutes don't bother to come at all. (*He turns to go, then turns back to Margaret*) Two minutes.

Hugh goes

There is a pause

Miriam (*amused at what has happened*) Well, what are you going to do, Margaret?
Margaret What can I do? I've never seen him like that before.
Maureen It's about time he turned on you. You've trod on him for years.
Miriam What's to happen about Mavis?
Margaret You heard what Hugh said. I'm not to have her.
Miriam You know what that means then, don't you?

Margaret Yes, of course I do. The thing is, does Hugh mean it?

Maureen I reckon you've got about another ninety seconds to find out.

Margaret (*to Maureen*) This is all your fault.

Maureen Mine?

Margaret If you'd had the good judgement not to have married a drunkard, none of this would have happened.

Maureen (*shouting*) She's starting again, Miriam, now you'd better warn her.

Miriam (*to Margaret*) It's not her fault.

Margaret He not only drinks himself now, he inflicts it on other people.

Maureen I didn't hear Hugh refuse too strongly when Desmond offered him.

Miriam This isn't going to get us anywhere.

Margaret You keep out of it.

Miriam Don't you tell me to keep out of it in my own house.

Margaret Hugh has never drunk before.

Maureen Well, if drinking's the reason for this sudden upper hand with you, it's a bloody pity he didn't start years ago.

Miriam and Maureen ad lib agreement

Margaret (*looking at them*) Oh, you're loving this aren't you, the two of you. I'm sure you're enjoying seeing me done out of my share of the money.

Maureen Well, yes, I am enjoying it. I can't deny it.

Margaret (*almost in tears*) It's not fair that you two should end up having it all.

Miriam Why not? We'll end up having Mavis.

Margaret I bet you've planned all this. I wouldn't be at all surprised if it had all been arranged. "How can we do her out of it." "Don't worry, leave it to me. I'll get Des to get him drunk. Load the bullets for him to fire."

Maureen Ooh, you're a bad bugger, Margaret.

Miriam It's not a bad idea, though. And if I'd thought of it first, I'd have done it, you take it from me.

Hugh (*off, screaming*) Margaret!

Maureen That's it, your time is up.

Margaret doesn't know what to do. She looks from Maureen to Miriam. She finally realizes she doesn't really have any alternative

In a flurry of temper and frustration, Margaret leaves the room

Maureen and Miriam look at each other and laugh heartily. Suddenly, Maureen screams with pain—the baby is on its way

Miriam What's the matter with you?

Maureen It's the baby. Better get Des.

Miriam doesn't move

Go on, get him quick.

Miriam rushes off. After a few seconds she returns with Tudor, Avril, Austin and Desmond

Miriam Are you all right?

Tudor Don't crowd round her. Let her have some air.

Maureen I haven't passed out. I've started labour that's all.

Miriam (*to Desmond*) You'd better get her back to the house.

Maureen I'm not having it there. I can't, not with all that scaffolding. Better take me straight to the hospital. Phone for an ambulance.

Miriam You might not have time.

Tudor I'll take her.

Avril Tudor'll take her, yes.

Miriam There you are, Maureen. Go with Tudor in the Reliant.

Maureen I think I'd rather wait for an ambulance.

Miriam Don't be silly. You'll be there in twenty minutes in the car.

Maureen It's Tudor you're talking about, mind. I'll probably end up having this baby in the back of that three-wheeler.

Austin Hey, if you do, and it's a boy, you can call him Robin.

Austin laughs but no-one else does

Sorry.

Miriam Come on, Maureen, let's get you up.

Miriam and Avril help Maureen to her feet

Fetch the car round, Tudor.

Tudor It's outside the front door.

Miriam Careful, now.

Miriam, Avril, Tudor and Austin ad lib as they get Maureen out of the room

Left alone, Mavis 2 gets up and goes and sits in the armchair

After a few seconds, Miriam and Austin enter

(*Entering*) She said she was feeling a bit funny earlier. (*She notices that Mavis 2 has moved. She goes to her*) I'm Miriam, Mavis. Do you remember me?

There is no reaction

Austin I still think you're making a big mistake.

Miriam How can you say that? I mean, look at her.

They both do

She's been here ten minutes and we haven't had a peep out of her yet. If this is how she's going to be, it's not a lot to put up with, especially when you think what we're going to get, now is it? And it's more now. Margaret has handed her lot in.

Austin She's not dull.

Miriam She was furious. Hugh wasn't having any of it. He put his foot down.

Austin Perhaps I should do the same.

Miriam Oh, look at her. You wouldn't send her back to that home would you? She's not going to be any trouble, I know it. Half the time you won't even know she's in the house.

Austin I still don't feel at ease somehow.

Miriam You're letting that business about my birthday party affect your judgement. She's changed, she's not the same as she was then. She's calmed down a lot. And you don't think they'd let her out of that place if she was dangerous, do you?

Austin But she's got a thing about me. She never liked me, not from the first.

Miriam Nonsense. Don't be paranoid. (*After a slight pause*) Having Mavis here is going to make quite a difference.

Austin You can say that again.

Miriam No, I mean financially. I mean, there's no reason now why you can't learn to drive. We could have a nice new car. Take a proper holiday.

Austin (*thinking this over*) A new car? Brand new?

Miriam Why not? We're talking about a lot of money.

Austin (*sitting on the arm of the chair*) I'd love a new car.

Miriam Well, there you are then. Just say the word and as soon as we've sold Father's house—you can have one.

Austin (*very tempted*) And I wouldn't even know she was in the house?

Miriam You wouldn't know now, if you couldn't see her.

Austin (*convinced*) Right. OK. We'll do it.

Miriam I knew you'd see reason. You won't be sorry.

Austin I'm sorry already.

Miriam I'll take her in the front room. Come on, Mavis. (*She helps her out of the chair*) Come with me. Let's go and see what's on the television, shall we?

Austin Miriam. (*She stops and looks at him*) Are you sure?

Miriam Of what?

Austin She's going to be all right, isn't she?

Miriam Trust me. (*She blows him a kiss*)

Miriam and Mavis exit

(Off, calling) Bring her case in will you Austin?

Austin goes to the suitcase and picks it up. It is heavier than he anticipated. He turns to leave the room, then stops. He is suspicious about the weight of the case. He lifts it up and down slightly. He is not happy. He places the case on the coffee-table, and after checking that he is not being watched, he opens it. Things seem normal at first but as he moves some of the clothing, he finds something. His expression turns to horror as he takes a huge hatchet from the case

Austin (*screaming*) Miriam!!!

Black-out

CURTAIN

FURNITURE AND PROPERTY LIST

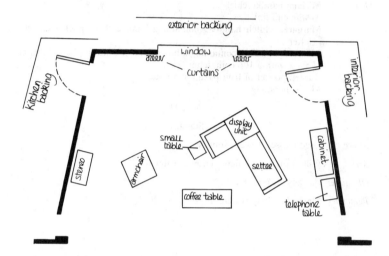

ACT I

SCENE 1

On stage: Stereo unit. *On it:* lamp
Armchair
Small table. *On it:* ashtray
Corner unit settee
Coffee-table. *On it:* ashtray
Wall cabinet. *In pull-down flap:* letter in an envelope, **Miriam**'s purse containing £10 note, credit card and £5 note. *On shelves:* glasses etc. *In cupboard section:* bottle of sherry, bottle of gin
Small table. *On it:* telephone, bowl of apples

Off stage: Hair-dryer, shampoo, towel, etc. **(Josey)**
Newspaper **(Austin)**
Cup of tea **(Austin)**
Tin of Carnation milk **(Austin)**

Personal: **Miriam:** handkerchief

SCENE 2

Strike: Cup of tea, newspaper

Set: Framed photograph for **Miriam**

Off stage: Pint of milk **(Maureen)**
             Carrier bag containing Star Wars electronic game **(Rupert)**
             2 hand towels **(Miriam)**
             Suitcase **(Mavis)**

Personal: **Miriam:** handkerchief
             Austin: cuff-links
             Margaret: clutch handbag containing handkerchief, pocket calculator,
                letter
             Maureen: handbag containing a box of matches and packet of cigarettes,
                purse with a 10p coin, letter
             Rupert: pocket of fruit pastilles in pocket
             Mavis: handbag

ACT II

SCENE 1

Strike: Used glasses, towels, suitcase

Set: Will in pull-down flap section of cabinet

Off stage: Car keys **(Margaret)**

Personal: **Mavis:** handbag containing strip of pills

SCENE 2

Strike: Will

Set: Dining-chair between settee and armchair
             Box of tissues, plate of almond cake on coffee-table

Off stage: Tray containing plate of corned beef and onion sandwiches, 5 cups and
                saucers, bowl of sugar, spoons, jug of milk, pot of tea **(Miriam)**
             Plate of pork pie **(Miriam)**
             Shopping trolley **(Austin)**
             Crateful of cider **(Desmond)**
             Bottle opener **(Austin)**

Personal: **Maureen:** handkerchief, handbag containing packet of cigarettes
             Margaret: handbag
             Desmond: lighted cigarette
             Tudor: broken set of the dentures in pocket
             Hugh: asthmatic pump

SCENE 3

Strike: Shopping trolley, all used glasses, crate of cider, bottle opener, tray of
             food, teapot, cups, saucers etc.

Set: Suitcase, **Mavis's** handbag

Off stage: Suitcase containing various clothes and a large hatchet **(Warden)**

Personal: **Tudor:** white hanky
             Mavis 2: handbag

LIGHTING PLOT

Practical fittings required: table lamp

Interior: a living-room. The same scene throughout

ACT I, SCENE 1. Late afternoon

To open: Dull, late afternoon effect

Cue 1	**Austin** can't believe his eyes. **Miriam** looks at him *Black-out*	(Page 15)

ACT I, SCENE 2. Evening

To open: Practical on with covering spots

Cue 2	**Mavis:** ". . . a merry Christmas to you all." *Black-out*	(Page 32)

ACT II, SCENE 1. Morning

To open: General daylight effect

Cue 3	**Mavis** blows a wet raspberry in **Margaret**'s face *Black-out*	(Page 45)

ACT II, SCENE 2. Day

To open: General daylight effect

Cue 4	**Tudor** turns to **Miriam** *Black-out*	(Page 58)

ACT II, SCENE 3. Afternoon

To open: General daylight effect

Cue 5	**Austin:** "Miriam!!!" *Black-out*	(Page 68)

EFFECTS PLOT

ACT I

MADE AND PRINTED IN GREAT BRITAIN BY
LATIMER TREND & COMPANY LTD, PLYMOUTH
MADE IN ENGLAND